To

Lin + Maggie

THE HILL
FARMER

Diolch o galon

xx

To my wonderful wife Rhian and children Siôr, Rolant and Mari, who make me tick; to Mum, Dad and my brother Huw, who gave me the best upbringing ever; and not forgetting all my family and friends, past and present, who have been there for me. Diolch o galon.

THE HILL
FARMER

Gareth Wyn Jones

with Elfyn Pritchard

First impression: 2014
Third impression: 2019

The publishers wish to acknowledge the support of
Cyngor Llyfrau Cymru

Cover design: Y Lolfa
Cover photograph: *The Hill Farm*, Indus for BBC Wales

ISBN: 978 178461 006 7

Published and printed in Wales
on paper from well-maintained forests by
Y Lolfa Cyf., Talybont, Ceredigion SY24 5HE
website www.ylolfa.com
e-mail ylolfa@ylolfa.com
tel 01970 832 304
fax 832 782

Contents

1

When Winter Came Late

White fury and media response

FRIDAY, 22 MARCH 2013, a week before Easter and a date engraved on my mind for ever, when a frightening freak snowstorm launched itself with great ferocity on large parts of Wales including the Carneddau, and the animals on the mountains were not prepared for it. The Carneddau are a group of mountains in Snowdonia, and form the largest contiguous area of high ground in Wales and England. They include the two highest peaks in Wales after Snowdon – Carnedd Dafydd and Carnedd Llywelyn – and my home, Ty'n Llwyfan, nestles below the lowest expanse of the mountains.

The summer of 2012 had been a dreadful one, and we farmers and our animals were not prepared for the harsh winter that was to follow. Our crops and silage were of poor quality and deficient in nutrients, so the sheep were not as strong as they should be – although we fed them concentrates to supplement their food in order to strengthen them for the coming months. To make matters worse, the bad summer was followed by a wet winter and, moreover, by March 2013, when the storm struck, the sheep were heavily pregnant, the main lambing period for us hill farmers being only days away.

And then on the Friday before Easter, the blizzard struck, causing great inconvenience to the whole family. Roads were blocked, the electricity was cut off, and in the howling gale and storm conditions off we went to ensure that the gates were open so that the sheep could move to the best places to withstand the onslaught. We have very good weather forecasts nowadays, and we had been warned that there was snow on the way, but had not been told of its intensity nor of the strength of the wind which made matters so much worse. The sheep instinctively went for shelter by the walls, normally the best position to shelter, but not when the wind is driving the snow into huge drifts in the very same sheltered places. This was the main reason for the problems we had, and not only us but hundreds of farmers throughout Wales, because the storm was widespread causing untold damage – drifting snow, sheds collapsing and electricity cut off for days on end, all the problems that a heavy and long-lasting snowstorm brings.

On Saturday we were digging for sheep in the huge drifts and, as I often do, I was tweeting and showing pictures on social media. I had a phone call from a local reporter for ITV, Ian Lang, asking if he could come along to film elements of our search for sheep. He came on Sunday morning and that was when he filmed the scene where I sank into a drift to look for a sheep. This short footage of film was shown time and time again on more than one TV channel as a vivid example of the seriousness of the situation in the hills of Wales.

Before the end of the day, the BBC had phoned requesting an interview; Channel Four did likewise, as well as Radio Cymru, Sky and Jason Mohammed for Radio Wales. We were in fact inundated with calls asking for interviews. And all this demand on my time really made life quite difficult because we were in a panic trying to save as many animals as we could.

This rush for interviews after the showing of just one brief clip of film underlines the power of the media; I realised that they offered a good opportunity to draw attention to the difficulties of farmers – especially those farming in the hills. It was also an opportunity to re-establish contact with the vast majority of the population, because I do believe that people are losing the connection with farming and the way food is produced. This would help us as an industry to share our problems with people through social media, so why not use it.

One of the first to venture up to the farm was Elen Wyn, a reporter for Welsh television, and although conditions were harsh, she really enjoyed it. We merely went about our business of rescuing animals and the cameras had to follow. During the day we came across a ewe ready to give birth and we asked her if she would like the opportunity to assist the sheep by pulling the lamb. She did, and she was absolutely delighted, and so we all were. Seeing new life being born gave us that extra push and incentive to save as many of our livestock as we could. Saving lives was the focus of all that I tried to do as a farmer in such a dark and desolate time for us all, with death all around. This made me feel a little bit better, and I also appreciated the presence of the camera crew because they were welcome company in what is usually a very lonely occupation. After all, a problem shared is a problem halved.

On the same day Matt Knight, an excellent film maker, came to the farm. He had rung me up the previous evening having seen my plight on the news, and asked if he could follow me with his camera during the day. He had been here before, filming *How to be Epic @ Everything* for CBBC. He followed me unobtrusively, keeping in the background, and produced a fantastic short film for YouTube called *Spring Disaster* which has had over 20,000 views and I feel very proud to be part of it.

And this kind of thing was a repeated experience for four or five days: different camera crews visiting, from John McGuire on *BBC Breakfast* to Andrew Davies from Channel 4. There were so many visitors I almost lost count, but made friends with many of them, and hopefully helped the farming industry as well.

What really brought the severity of the situation home to me during this period of a week or so was to witness one of the ponies we have on the Carneddau giving birth to a foal – a foal that died because of the bad weather. But that pony stood above the dead foal guarding him for four days, and I took a picture of it and tweeted Alun Davies the agriculture minister in the

Assembly Government. I asked him permission for farmers to be allowed to bury their dead on the farms, because there is a European ruling against burying dead animals on farmland.

It was the week before Easter, and the Minister was on holiday, so we had to wait until the following Tuesday before he could deal with the situation and convey his decision to us. I thought that the least he could do was give us permission because we could not get a lorry up to the farm to collect the dead bodies, nor could we move from here ourselves, and the same situation faced large numbers of other farmers as well. Interviews on various TV programmes and channels, and numerous demands from the farming community all combined to put pressure on him, and eventually he agreed, and permission was given for burial on farms in some areas for a limited period.

This was vital because we were in the lambing season and this was such a devastating freak storm that no one could have prepared for it. My father is 77 but he doesn't ever remember having weather like this on the Carneddau, so much snow so late in the season. As I previously mentioned, one of the reasons for such great losses was that the ewes were heavily pregnant or had just given birth, and the ponies likewise. It was an atrocious time for us to have to go looking for struggling animals. I had my gun on my shoulder as I combed the whole area, and if I dug two sheep out of the snow I had to make an on-the-spot decision as to which one was the stronger of the two for me to carry down to the farm, because I could only carry one at a time. So the other one had to be shot because in the time it took me to carry one to safety and return to the same spot, the crows would have pecked out the eyes of the other and bitten her tongue off. There were difficult decisions to be made, decisions which I will take with me to my grave. Maybe I didn't get all of them right; my only consolation is that I did my best, and I couldn't have done more.

Today, looking back, I'm glad that I was filmed in such a dramatic situation. People often insinuate that the Welsh put a stretch on things in order to better the story, and that farmers in general are always complaining even when there is no cause to. But no one can dispute such clear documentary evidence showing the terrible crisis that had arisen. It hopefully gave the general public an insight into what we do as an industry. Mind you, once you stick your head above the parapet you're in danger of being shot, and I had lots who verbally attacked me – on Twitter for example – accusing me of cruelty in leaving the sheep out in such weather instead of having them in the shed, and leaving the ponies on the mountain in such inclement weather. There is a blog called 'Oscar's theories' and some comments on that blog were just horrible. Comments made by people who obviously didn't understand that there is a clue to the kind of farming we do in our names – we are hill farmers, we farm on the hills and we don't bring our sheep in for lambing, that is why the lambing season is late so that the sheep usually have the best weather possible. Usually this happens, but not in 2013! But you've got to take it on the chin and luckily I am thick-skinned enough, but it must be remembered that we all have feelings too. I like to be thought of as a good person doing his best, and there is nothing worse than someone sticking a knife in your back. But that's life, and if you put yourself in front of the camera you've got to be ready for quite a lot of nit-picking.

As if the hassle with the weather wasn't enough, we as a family had agreed to take part in a twelve-month occupational documentary – *The Hill Farm* – produced by a Cardiff-based TV company called Indus. It wasn't an easy decision to make because all the television work I had done previously was just about me. I had taken part in *Snowdonia 1890*, *Young Farmer of the Year*, *Fferm Ffactor*[1] and other programmes, but now I

---

1   *Fferm Ffactor*. A Welsh language series on S4C showing a dozen farmers competing against each other in farming related tasks, with an elimination process reducing the final number to three, and eventually to an outright winner. See Chapter 9.

was opening a different door and asking other members of my family to get involved. But the basic reason for finally accepting was to ensure that there would hopefully be a future for hill farming, that there would be farmers on the mountains after we had long gone. I honestly believe that we are a dying breed and that family farms could become a relic of the past. Hopefully the series of four programmes would present an honest picture of farming on the Carneddau.

I was born on 5 May 1967, and on that day BBC Wales transmitted a programme called *Shepherds of Moel Siabod*, a beautiful piece of filming, a programme which captured an era, a fantastic piece of history, and thankfully the family depicted in the film is still farming the area shown. I hope that *The Hill Farm* will be just as good and will make people respect our way of life, and respect us for being Welsh.

As an industry I believe we are excellent at producing the goods, but we are bloody rubbish at selling them. And it is largely our own fault, we have not endeared ourselves to the general public, and there still exists the stereotyped picture of a farmer as a man standing on top of the mountain with a stick in his hand shouting 'get off my land'.

Others regard us as scroungers with begging bowls in our hands looking to Europe for sustenance, and raking in the grants as fast as we can, sitting in front of the fire waiting for that cheque to drop on the mat. Sorry, but that is a completely false picture. The farmers I know are hard-working people, doing a good job producing high quality food. And it is a young man's game. Sadly we are a dying breed. I am 47 and one of the youngest farmer on the Carneddau. I have been made chairman of the Aber and Llanfairfechan Grazing Committee and from my chair I gaze at the other members sitting before me. No young faces. They are all ageing. Where will the next generation come from?

Hopefully *The Hill Farmer* will have made people realise that when they walk into a grocer's shop or the butcher's and buy Welsh produce, Welsh lamb for instance, that they are buying part of the family which produced it. Not just me but all farmers. We must make people realise that the hills and mountains look as they do because of the farmers and the farming that goes on there, and that it is very hard work. Farmers help to retain the balance in nature, and foxes are a good example of how this is done. Yes, foxes are beautiful creatures, but you get good-looking serial killers, as well. No one wants to kill all foxes, but unless their numbers are kept down the balance in the countryside goes, and it isn't just the farms that suffer, but nature itself. Unless foxes are contained there will be a death of ground-nesting birds, for example. Farmers do these thankless jobs without complaining, but of course there is benefit for us as well: the more foxes that are killed, the less the number of lambs killed by them. Nature conservationists who want to protect everything often fail to understand that there needs to be a balance. Eighty per cent of people today live in towns and cities and other built-up areas; to a large extent they have lost contact with nature, with the countryside and the way it works, and the way food is produced. At the end of the day these are the people who put crosses in boxes to elect politicians. It is so important for us to open our farm gates, let the people in to see what we are doing, to explain and educate, and this is another reason why I go on television – to explain what happens. You cannot just depend on politicians and on schools to present a fair picture. People have lost contact with the countryside; they need to understand that milk comes from cows and that burgers are not pulled from thin air but are processed from meat, and that the meat comes from cattle, sheep and pigs. These people are our customers and we can't afford to lose them. If we lose the countryside we lose the farmers and no food will be produced. We can import of course, but only in the near future. As the world population increases, food production needs to increase to feed the world... well, need I say more?

A couple of weeks after the snow had gone we buried

76 ponies, bringing the total to over a hundred. This was devastation, an important piece of the history of the Carneddau gone for ever. My father always maintains that the ponies are there for a reason, and have been there since time immemorial. However, to look on the bright side of disaster, it can be said that the snow and the terrible weather we had was, in a way, a natural culling process, because what it did was take out of the stock the old and the weak and the unhealthy, leaving the rest of the flock stronger. It was nevertheless a staggering experience, as the snow cleared, to see clusters of dead ponies here and there on the mountain. It underlined the full extent of the tragedy that had befallen us. That is when I started in earnest to consider what had happened and strived to make sense of it all. But it made me sad, and Rhian my wife says she could tell by my voice how I felt when I talked about burying all these ponies in two burial sites. It was a harrowing experience. As farmers we often appear rough and ready, and people tend to think that we have no feelings. Nothing could be further from the truth.

What made the experience worse was that the ponies could not be buried where they had died. They had gone to sheltered areas, which were important archaeological sites. The burial locations had to be selected carefully, and the ponies carried there in truckloads. Not a pleasant task.

During the whole time it was very physical, very emotional, very tiring, but when you are in the middle of a crisis you have to try to control your feelings and make decisions which, on contemplation, perhaps you will regret. But the main aim always is to look after the living, because it is the living that secures the future, and it's the living that pays the bills. I am, hopefully, as a result of this experience, a better person, a stronger person, and walking into the kitchen at the end of a long, tiring day, seeing my wife and my healthy children there, gave me the strength to carry on the next day.

Recognition

After the snow had finally melted away, I received a phone call to say that I had been nominated for an award – the NFU/Principality Community Champion of Wales! Three people were nominated and the phone call was to request an interview with Pat Ashman, Principality's sponsorship and events manager, the NFU's Dafydd Jarret and Stephen James, the deputy chairman of the NFU. All three came up to the farm for a chat and it was revealed that I had been nominated because of all the promotional work I had done, during the snow, to bring the plight of farmers and their animals to the public's notice.

I was nominated by Janet Finch-Saunders, A.M. for Aberconwy, who wrote:

> Millions of people watched Mr Jones's plight and his amazing efforts to rescue dozens of pregnant ewes and Carneddau ponies trapped on the mountain following the tragic circumstances brought about by the severe weather in north Wales. He inspired the community of Llanfairfechan to help farmers in the area.

Later, the whole family was invited to the Royal Welsh Show site in Llanelwedd and we all had a fantastic reception. We were ushered to the reception office and Mari, our youngest, kept whispering: 'Dad is going to win, isn't he?' I didn't really think I had a hope in hell, and it came as quite a shock when my name was announced as the winner. I was really lost for words when I received the award; I never really prepare a speech and didn't think that I would need one on this occasion. I was a bit gobsmacked. But I realised it was a great opportunity to speak up for the farming community: the press were there, the television cameras were there, all these people in the same room at the same time. So I went up to the dais, thanked my wife and my children and my family, and then I went on my high horse about the selling of local produce and urging people to support locally produced food. Buy Welsh – buy British, this was the message and it went down very well.

I have been lucky in my aim to promote our industry because I have known the right people, and met them at the right time. The NFU had a promotion to buy locally and most people I have met in the media – not all, the odd one wants to stick a knife in you – were most positive in their attitude. You can't please all of the people all of the time, but if you are honest and truthful most people will respect you for it. They might not agree with you all the time but they will respect you. So it was a great feeling to win, and to receive a cheque for £500 and a lovely slate clock. But the title was worth more than the money or the clock. The other two short-listed nominees were Jonathan Harrington from Powys and Gerwyn Owen from Ceredigion, both worthy winners.

Following the terrible winter of 2013, we had a fantastic summer, and everybody was feeling good because of the sun. We even made some small bales of hay, taking us back a few years in our haymaking. Going back to my childhood, really.

And then one day I had a phone call from someone at the *Farmers Weekly* office, inviting me and my wife to attend a celebratory event at the Grosvenor Hotel in London. The theme for the night was 'James Bond – Licence to Thrill', so I had to find a tuxedo and had to book a hotel. I started surfing the web and had the shock of my life when I saw the prices for accommodation at London hotels. I really had second thoughts about going. So I phoned a very good friend of mine, Chris Hamilton who works for Carrs Billington Agricultural Merchants, to say what my problem was. 'Leave it with me Jones,' he said, 'I've got friends in high places,' and in three days he phoned back. 'I've got you into the Grosvenor,' he said, 'and you don't pay anything.' He had asked the boss of Norbrook's, Edward Haughey, to sponsor me. So it was a train down to London for Rhian and me, and a taxi to the Grosvenor, and I've never seen splendour like it.

The ceremony wasn't held until the evening, so we went walkabout and found ourselves in a shop where I bought a sports jacket for £300, the most expensive jacket I've ever had but, as Rhian said, I needed something to note the occasion.

On the way back we passed an Aston Martin garage and decided to call in, and as we entered we could smell the leather of the new cars. It was a beautiful place and there was a brand-new black Aston Martin in the window and a well dressed man sitting at a desk nearby. So I went up to him and asked if I could sit in the car to experience what it felt like. 'Oh no,' he said, 'I'm sorry, that was sold yesterday.' I turned to Rhian and said to her, in Welsh naturally: 'We'll be sitting in that car within five minutes.' So I started talking to him and when he asked me where we were from and what we were doing in London, I said we were down for the *Farmers Weekly* award ceremony and staying at the Grosvenor Hotel. And I asked him if he knew that the Aston Martin company started by producing tractors, and we spoke about buying British and how I was keen to promote home-produced food and Welsh lamb. 'Do you know what,' he said, 'I'll go and get them keys and you can have a sit in the car.' So I got to sit in the car and Rhian took a picture and I tweeted it all over. It was an amazing day for us.

After we got back to the hotel and changed for the evening, we went down to meet Edward Haughey for drinks. He wasn't going to be at the ceremony because he had another meeting. Then we went to meet the others, including quite a few Welsh people: John Foulkes and his wife; Richard and Rhian Parry of Crugeran, son Harri Parry (a finalist) and his fiancée (now wife) Elin. Then we went through to the ballroom for the reception and dinner. The seating arrangements for the dinner were posted on a large board, and we couldn't for the life of us find our names. We met Edward Bailey of the NFU and Emyr Jones of FUW, but I started panicking, beginning to think that I wasn't supposed to be there, because the other guests were going off to their tables.

A beautifully dressed lady came by and greeted me by my first name. 'I'm Debbie,' she said, and I had no idea who Debbie was, but she knew me, and this often happens. (I've been on television and had my picture in the newspapers and people know my face – whilst I've hardly moved from Ty'n Llwyfan to meet people. So they have the advantage over me.) Debbie worked for the *Farmers Weekly* and she said that the reason my name wasn't down was because we were both, Rhian and I, to sit at the top table.

This came as a bit of a shock, and as we went towards the table we met a large Scottish farmer who came up to me and said: 'Hello, laddie, got to shake your hand. Loved the job you did for the farmers. Fantastic. Well done you!' It was a good feeling to be shaken by the hand by a fellow Celt who accepted that I'd done a good job.

Then we went to our table, and one of the people there was Lord Plumb of whom I had heard my father speaking when I was young. He was NFU President in the 1970s and 1980s. Also present was one of the chiefs of Defra, and one of the owners of the *Farmers Weekly*. It was a great feeling to be amongst them. The guest speaker was Kate Silverton, the BBC news presenter. Ed Bailey and Emyr Jones were on the next table, one down from the top table, and there was much leg-pulling, as you can imagine.

It was a proud moment for me and Rhian, to be given a special mention for work done for the farming community. So after the formal dinner was over we danced away the hours, and all of it costing us nothing. We didn't have to spend a single penny thanks to Edward Haughey, and it was sad to learn of his father's death in a helicopter crash a few months later.

I have no doubt that there were many farmers in Wales who had been in the same or even worse predicament than me during the terrible weather; the only difference was that there was a camera and radio crew following me. Sometimes in life it is who you know, not what you know, that counts, and being in the right place at the right time. When that happens you've got to make the most of it.

And so 2013 ended on a happy note, but I will never forget that year's spring and Mother Nature's ferocious attack on man and beast.

2

Childhood and Youth

Hello Mrs Robinson!

ALTHOUGH I AM a farmer, the most important aspect of my education was not acquired on the farm, or in the schools I attended, but in Pendyffryn Caravan Park and Mrs Robinson was my teacher! The site was bought by my grandfather in 1954 and it has remained in the family ever since. It is situated on the outskirts of Penmaenmawr on the side of the A55 and has on-site static caravans, mobiles and tents, and it played an unforgettable part in my education when I was young.

During the summer holidays, in the early 1980s, when I was about 13 years old, I used to go to Pendyffryn every morning with my cousins, Owen John and Ieuan, to round up the cattle ready for Uncle Wil to milk them, and then to work in the caravan park. My cousins were older than me, Owen John was 18 and Ieuan 16.

We shared the tasks of emptying the bins and cleaning the toilets and shower cubicles; Owen cleaned the toilets, thank goodness for that; Ieuan did the brushing and I attended to the wash basins and scoured them clean with Vim.

The park was full to capacity for most of the summer, every static occupied and many caravans stopping for a night or two, with the tent area a bright pattern of colour and almost every available space occupied. People came from all over, from Germany and France and other European countries, as well as all parts of Britain.

One morning in particular stands out in my mind, a fine

summer morning, and the three of us were hard at it cleaning the service area. We always instinctively cleaned the Gents side of the building first, being rather shy to enter the Ladies' toilets and showers. But it had to be done, and Ieuan, the most confident of the three of us, was the one who knocked on the door every morning and shouted: 'Anybody there?' If there was no answer we would enter and strive to clean the whole area as quickly as we could before anyone came in.

On this particular morning Owen was busy in the toilets, Ieuan brushing in one of the cubicles and I was cleaning the basins with Vim and vigour when two women, obviously a mother and daughter, came in, chatting in a foreign tongue which I guessed to be French. The mother was in her 40s and the daughter in her teens and both were good-lookers.

They had come for a shower, and we would have gone from there and left them to it had they asked us. But they didn't, they ignored us completely, placed their bags on the floor and started to undress round the corner from where we were, but Ieuan and I could see their bare bottoms in the mirror. Owen continued with the cleaning whilst Ieuan and I looked at each other. I'm sure that our eyes were popping out of our heads, and the sink which I happened to be cleaning at the time had an extra scrubbing that morning.

Thankfully, the two stepped inside the cubicles shortly afterwards and nothing could be seen or heard except water splashing. But there was worse – or better – to come! Soon both came out chatting and laughing and proceeded to towel themselves in front of us as if we were invisible. Were they perhaps saying things about us, making fun of us perhaps for pretending that we couldn't see them? That was quite true because Ieuan and I were looking at each other not knowing what to do, wanting to look and yet...! I was an innocent country lad, never having seen such a sight and not knowing then what 'striptease' meant. But that is what we had. And I still remember it well, and the three of us continue to remind ourselves occasionally of that morning when I learnt quite a bit about naked bodies – naked ladies, at least!

As summer followed summer and I grew older, the caravan park became a great place for a teenager. There was no need to go to the youth club to look for a girl; there were girls aplenty visiting the park every year, for weekends and for longer periods – each one, or so I imagined, looking for a boyfriend from the farming community. We were sturdy lads brought up on hard physical work and were very fit, and because I had blond hair, I liked to think that I was attractive to the ladies. Well, there must have been something in it, for I never found it difficult to get a new girlfriend.

Working in the caravan park was indeed an education in itself. But it was my encounter with a married woman, not seeing naked women or acquiring new girlfriends every week, which taught me most. She was staying in one of the static caravans and I must not in fairness reveal her true identity as someone might remember her, so I'll refer to her as Mrs Robinson – for obvious reasons. Obvious to me, at any rate!

She called out to me one morning when I was passing to say that her gas bottle was empty and asked for a replacement. I went into the shop to get a new one and after fixing it Mrs Robinson asked me if I fancied a cup of coffee. And so I innocently entered the caravan for my coffee. My two cousins had gone on to Baclaw farm in Conwy by then and I, having finished my work on the site, had an hour or two to spare. And I spent the rest of the morning in the caravan. Mrs Robinson was quite a character and offered much more than coffee, and it wasn't biscuits either. She was in fact an excellent teacher and I learnt more during that two-hour period with her than in previous or subsequent years. The curtains were drawn and I was educated in the semi-darkness, but lack of daylight was no problem. It is best perhaps that I also draw a veil over that morning's proceedings!

Tamazin and me

My connection with another female, Tamazin, was much more innocent. Not surprising really because we were both only five years old at the time. Ty'n Llwyfan, my home for many years now, was originally two houses which my father let to two families whilst we as a family lived in a cottage on the yard. Two Germans lived in one of the houses and my father's cousin Bill – Bill Gwyndy as he was called – lived in the other one with his wife Ann and his four children: Liam, Geraint, Tamazin and Bleddyn. Tamazin was the same age as me, whilst Bleddyn, two years younger, was the same age as my brother Huw.

In the early 1970s my father built a new cottage nearby and we children frequently went there to pry and to see the building work. One day, having seen the painters busy on the house and being keen to help, Tamazin and I decided to paint the garage. She somehow got hold of a tin of black-lead, and so we proceeded to make a huge mess in the garage and on ourselves, until the walls and our clothes were black. I don't remember much about the incident, apart from the shock we had when we were severely chastised for what we had done, and that for trying to help! My father was furious. Traces of the black-lead can still be seen in the garage and I have a little giggle when I see it and when I gaze occasionally at the photo of me and Tamazin looking so innocent!

Rallying

As I grew older, for a period driving became more important than anything else in my life. Farmers' sons are lucky because driving is part and parcel of their world, as cars and tractors are a regular feature on all farms, so that most farm children are proficient drivers long before reaching the statutory age for driving. Farmers' sons learn by driving in the yard and in the fields. But at one stage we were not content merely with ordinary driving – for an afternoon we became rally drivers! It was late June, harvest time, with little bales in the hayfields. I was 15 and my brother Huw – Huw Bach as I call him – was 13.

One day we were at Gerlan Farm in Llanfairfechan, the traditional home of the family and where Uncle Huw and Auntie Ann lived. A young lad, slightly older than me and my brother, lived and worked on the farm at the time, and he owned a Mini and was quite a skilful rally driver. He was Nigel Mulliner, a Welsh-speaking Welshman, in spite of his name, and on this particular day all three of us were working in the same field whilst my father and his brothers were in another.

We placed the bales as obstacles for the rallying, and away went Nigel in his little Mini, weaving in and out between the bales, and performing handbrake turns on the corners. Then he repeated his act in Uncle Wil's Capri. This was a big brown 1600 car, and I had my turn after Nigel, but didn't get on very well although I tried to copy Nigel's tricks.

'My turn now Gar,' said my little brother, but it was decided that Uncle Wil's Capri was too big and too powerful for him. However, Dad's car was in the yard, a green metallic Escort, number GCC 520N, and it was agreed that it would be all right for Huw to have a go in that because it was so much smaller. Away he went, but as he attempted to negotiate the corner at the bottom of the field, trying to emulate Nigel's handbrake turn, he drove bonnet first into the ditch until the car was covered in mud and was completely stuck.

It proved impossible for the three of us to move it, so we had to fetch the tractor to pull it free. By this time Dad and his brothers had arrived to see what had happened. He was furious, although there was nothing wrong with the car. He thought the world of the car, he almost worshipped it and so Huw Bach would have copped it right and proper had he been anywhere near, but he was wise enough to run away and hide in his bedroom. By the time Dad arrived home he had quietened down a bit and as a result, and the fact that

23

Mam sided with Huw, he got out of it better than he could have hoped.

The rallying period didn't last long – the beginning and the end came the same day thanks to Huw – but I learnt an important lesson. If I happened to do something wrong in the future, the best plan would be to keep away from my father until he had cooled down, and also get my mother to side with me, of course!

Glynllifon

By the end of the 1980s I had attended Llanfairfechan Infant School, Pant y Rhedyn Primary School and Ysgol Tryfan, the Welsh secondary school in Bangor, and had arrived at Glynllifon Agricultural College, growing up fast but still a bit mad – because one night I could have met my Maker.

There were a good number of us Welsh youths together in the college, from the Llŷn Peninsula, from Anglesey and along the coast as far as Conwy, and I lived on the border between those who went to Glynllifon and those who went to Llysfasi. I well remember Bryn Bodeidda, Robin Trebedda, Edward Ty'n Llan, Paul Bach, and John Bach Bodnithod – a proper raver, and many more.

We would frequently go for a pint on Wednesday evenings, to Caernarfon or a pub somewhere in the vicinity, and one night some of us were in town and missed the last bus back to the college. Luckily, one of the girls, Anwen, was with us, and she had come in her Mini, so the rest of us had a lift back with her. We were all chatting and showing off as lads do, because she was quite a beauty and the beer was talking. When we arrived at the courtyard where we were staying, Anwen dropped us off, but John Bach stayed for a moment to talk to her. The Mini has no boot, only a fairly wide fender at the back, and whilst John was talking to her I did a very silly thing. I stood on the fender and leant forward to grab the roof of the car.

The next moment she took off without knowing that I was there, and she drove like mad round the corners. As she rounded the last corner I fell off and rolled about on the uneven stones of the courtyard.

Beer is a good anaesthetic, but I knew that I had hurt my knee and I went straight to bed without looking at it and immediately fell asleep. But when I woke up I was in agony and could hardly walk. We had an important test in the field that morning, laying a length of fencing, and Glyn who was responsible for us noticed that there was something amiss and insisted on knowing what was wrong. He was startled when he saw my knee with all the skin scraped away from it and he immediately sent me to see the nurse. She naturally wanted to know what had happened, but I didn't tell her the truth. I said that I had tripped and fallen, but she obviously suspected that there was more to it than that.

It was a miracle that nothing worse happened, larking about could have had serious consequences because near where I had fallen were big trees and large boulders. Had I struck one of those it could have been curtains for me. Young lads, beer and cars do not mix, and that was an important lesson for me to learn.

One Saturday Night

If things could have been worse for me in Glynllifon, then things could also have been much worse for me one Saturday night 20 years ago. I break out in a sweat every time I think about it.

It was in the days when just about everyone had long hair. We met up in the local pub for a pint before going on the town in Bangor. I was Rhian's boyfriend by this time and she lived in Upper Bangor, her mother and the girls having moved from their farm in Anglesey. So I was lucky, I had a place to stay the night and didn't have to find a taxi to take me home.

One Saturday night five of us, members of the family and friends, had met prior to proceeding to Bangor: me and brother Huw, cousin Richard and two of our best friends, Mark Hughes and Jason Jones. Two good lads! Another one, Steve Bach, arrived, Steve Flatfoot as we used to call him. That meant six of us and that was a problem. I had a little Volkswagen, the Beetle, which carried five at a pinch, three in the back and two in the front, but six – never!

'You'll have to go on the bus,' I told Steve, because he had been the last to arrive.

'Don't leave me behind,' he said in an appealing voice. 'I'll travel in the boot. I'm small enough.'

But the Beetle has no boot as the engine is in the back, but there was some room in the front, under the bonnet and Steve was pushed into the confined space. He could sit on a little step and lean forward so that we could close the cover. It would be a most uncomfortable journey for him, but he opted for it rather than taking the bus.

Away we went towards Bangor, each one of us smoking and chatting, making silly remarks as is the wont of young lads. As we approached Gypsy Corner near Talybont, Mark suddenly said: 'Shouldn't we give Steve a shout?'

'Why?' I asked.

'Do you know that this car can float on water?'

'What do you mean?' I asked.

'It's airtight,' he said. 'Back and front.'

Lord, what a panic. An airtight car and Steve trapped underneath the bonnet. We were on the open road with nowhere to pull over, so we started shouting at Steve at the top of our voices, but there was no reply. Near Talybont there was a bus stop and we drew in there and Huw my brother jumped from the car like a shot and opened the bonnet.

'Oh, are we in Bangor already?'

Steve's voice! What a relief. He hadn't heard us shouting because the tyres on the road made so much noise. He was perfectly all right; thank heavens for that, all of us having been afraid that his face would be blue. He could easily have suffocated. It makes you think doesn't it how foolish you can be.

I have been lucky in life to have had good friends over the years, many of them close relatives as well as friends. I'm also one of a big family and that is more important than anything.

3

Our Family

I AM THE secretary of our farming company – Owen Jones and Sons – a family company of eight members, four brothers and four sons. It was established by Owen Jones, my grandfather on my father's side, and he died when my father was 26, before I was born. My grandmother also died young, and so did my grandfather on my mother's side.

I am convinced that the premature death of my grandfather drew the family together, the sons at least. There were four of them in the company at first, and at my grandfather's funeral my father overheard two farmers talking, with one of them saying:

'It will be interesting to see which farm will go first.'

Dad returned home and told the other three brothers what he had heard. They were only young and there was a heavy load on their shoulders, but they stayed together, closed ranks and not a single farm was sold, and so they remained until we – four sons of the four brothers – joined them to form the company of eight.

We are all Joneses in the company: Dad and me, Ty'n Llwyfan, Llanfairfechan, and the three brothers and their sons: Tecwyn (Teg) Plas Ucha, Penmaenmawr, and his son Robert; Huw Gerlan, Llanfairfechan, and Owen John the son; and William Roger, Henblas, Llanfairfechan, and his son Ieuan. Usually most of us meet for a cuppa every morning in my father's home, the bungalow at Ty'n Llwyfan, to discuss matters relating to the company, and to decide, when the need arises, on our work schedule for the day.

Considering all the quarrelling and disagreements within families today, it is fair to ask how we, a company of eight from two different generations, can pull together so well. Someone often asks my father: 'Do you quarrel?' And he has a stock answer to the question: 'No, our farms are big enough so we never tread on each other's toes.' But that's not the real reason. We have a mutual respect for each other, and the cousins are more like brothers and friends than cousins. We often argue and disagree, but we don't quarrel, and continue to be friends. Moreover we, the younger members, hold the older generation in great respect. I only remember one grandmother, because the other one and the two grandfathers died before I was born, so I am greatly dependant on my father and his brothers who are with us every day.

I learned much from them because each one is different with different skills. Uncle Huw is a good mechanic always repairing something, and I enjoyed helping him on Saturdays when I was young. Uncle Wil can turn his hand to almost anything. He used to do the majority of the milking in the family but he is also a good builder, good with electricity, and game to have a go at anything. Uncle Teg is a good herdsman and shepherd, with a flock of sheep as good as any in the country, and his knowledge of earmarks is unsurpassed. I learned so much from all of them and the sons follow their fathers in their interests and skills.

It is definitely like father, like son, in my case, being responsible for the paperwork of the company as my father once was, and more of an all-rounder than a specialist, liking sheepdogs, restless, on the go all the time, garrulous, but not as garrulous as him!

My father's opinion of me

What you see is what you get, that's Gareth. He is the company secretary and he's a good one, the work nowadays taking up on average two days a week. He is also the organiser, assuming command for the day's work and deciding on chores to be completed. If he says we'll meet at six in the morning, he'll be there at six, and he'll expect us to be there as well!

He is an excellent sheepdog trainer. I gave him a dog and a pony when he was young in order to foster his love of farming. And it worked!

When he grew older he was given a bigger pony, because Carneddau ponies are small, and he was a big tall lad. One day I had occasion to ride his pony, and when we came to a wall the pony immediately jumped over it. That's when I realised that Gareth had been secretly training it to jump and had set up fences and obstacles for the purpose, and that without anyone's knowledge!

He is a very socially-minded person, and this aspect of his personality finds outlet in his work as a local councillor and as an ex-mayor of Llanfairfechan (2011–12).

My father is a great believer in family succession. He brought me up to be a farmer and he is at the moment working on Siôr, our eldest son. When Siôr was ten he bought him 30 hens, and he sells eggs and buys more hens with the profit. Siôr and his grandparents are great mates, and his grandmother helps him to clean the eggs before they are sold.

The importance of succession is one thing that keeps us together, but there is another element also, the women in our lives. I like to think that there are traces of my grandmother's (Nain) characteristics in me as well as my father's – mainly seriousness, depth and feeling. It is our wives who feed us, and this also keeps us together. I'm sure that I'll be condemned for saying it, especially by those who believe that men and women should be equal, and that equality means sameness. Work on hill farms is a constant toil, hard and demanding, and we often work long hours in inclement and inhospitable weather, and during shearing and sheep gathering times there can be as many as ten or twelve of us wanting lunch and tea. We have no time to prepare it ourselves, so that work is done by the women.

That is a fact, and it is their nutritional food and care that keeps us fit for hard work.

It isn't only their diligence that keeps us together but the fact that not one of them wants more than any of the others. Not a single one of them has big ideas, fancying a smart car or expensive clothes from London boutiques. Thankfully, there is no jealousy between the families because any aspect of that would create chaos within the company.

Dad has another brother who is not a member of the company, Robert – Uncle Bobby, the eldest brother who was brought up by his grandparents and who farms Coed Hywel, Bangor, with his son, Robert Tudur, and his grandson Dewi Lloyd. We have a close relationship with them as well, Tudor being the chairperson of the Grazing Society (2012) of which we are all members, and his sister Eleri is one of Rhian's closest friends. It is nice to be a member of a large family, and things don't end there either, because many second cousins are also farmers in the area.

I learned most of what I know about farming and about life in general from my father. He has numerous stories and memories of people now dead, and these are transferred from generation to generation, teaching us a lot in the process. He has told us many times about the farmer who said there would be a penny on his coffin lid at his funeral and that anyone who felt that he owed them something could take it. The coffin was lowered into the grave with the penny still on it.

He also tells us often about the hardships of life in the past and about a small-holder named Robert Thomas who lost a cow – a great loss to a small farmer – and said about his smallholding that night: 'Thank God the darkness has come to hide the bloody place.'

Land and property are not the only important things that should be transferred from generation to generation: beliefs, stories and sayings of those who have gone before us are also important, and are part and parcel of what holds us together as one big family.

Meeting Rhian

As I mentioned in the last chapter, a few of us youths used to go to Bangor on Saturday nights, often travelling on the bus or a minibus and returning home by taxi. One of the places we frequented there was the Octagon club and on this particular Saturday night, when I saw Rhian for the first time, my cousin Ieuan was with us. The usual pattern was to go round the Bangor pubs prior to arriving at the Octagon later on.

Sometime during the evening I saw Ieuan chatting to a group of girls, and Rhian was amongst them. I didn't talk to her that night but she had caught my eye. She's a pretty girl I thought to myself, but had no chance to say a few words to her before the taxi arrived and it was time to go home.

Ieuan wasn't with us the following Saturday, indeed only two of us turned up in the pub in Llanfairfechan prior to going to Bangor, 'Mike the bike' and me. We were not prepared to pay for a taxi just for the two of us, and so Mike said he'd go on the motorbike and that I could go with him.

He had a very powerful machine, and it was doing well over 100 m.p.h and I felt as sick as a parrot. In fact I hate motorbikes and this was the first and last time I have ever been on one.

Mike went to meet his girlfriend and I went to the Octagon, and yes, the girl I'd fancied was there. I summed up courage to talk to her and I must confess, although I don't think a farmer should admit this, but it was love at first sight for me!

I spent the rest of the evening in her company, but I didn't have a lift home because Mike was with his girlfriend, and I mentioned this to Rhian. She said that her parents had gone to the cinema and that they would take me home. So, on the first night that I met Rhian, I was taken home by her parents – a fine start to a loving relationship! And her father still remembers the occasion and her mother well remembers my first visit to their home in Anglesey.

Me through the eyes of my father-in-law

I knew Gareth's father, or at least I knew of him, before I met Gareth. I farmed in Llangwyllog on Anglesey and went with my father every year to the important sheep sale at Aber, near Llanfairfechan, a sale held by Bob Parry Auctioneers. 'Rol,' Gareth's father, was a dominant figure in that sale and everyone there became immediately aware of his presence when he arrived. Aber sheep were considered always to be of a very high standard.

But taking Gareth home was my first visit to Ty'n Llwyfan, the family home. Having three daughters I was often their taxi, and I was fetching Rhian from the Octagon – the old County Theatre – one Saturday night, and Gareth was stuck for a lift. He had come there on a motorbike but his friend had gone with his girlfriend, and Gareth had no lift home. So there was nothing for it but to take him to Llanfairfechan in the Cortina. I had never seen him before, and this was a strange beginning indeed to a love affair, the father- and mother-in-law taking the future son-in-law home on the night of their first date!

I have worked a lot with the family since then, especially at Plas Newydd, the farm their company rents on Anglesey. They are a large family and there are always many people in Ty'n Llwyfan – large family, big business and good farmers.

Rhian has been very lucky, and so have I, fortunate in my three sons-in-law and in my grandchildren, including Gareth and Rhian's three – Siôr, Rolant and Mari Non, the three very different from each other, and the middle one, Rolant, very much like me.

Me through my mother-in-law's eyes

I didn't notice him much the night we took him home from the Octagon, but I well remember the first time he came to our house. We lived on a farm in Llangwyllog on Anglesey, but I was the only one at home at the time. It was a fine Sunday afternoon, and I can see him now, coming through the door, shoulder length blond hair and blue, blue eyes. He was very handsome to tell the truth, in his colourful Bermuda shorts with shirt to match. He obviously knew all about colour coordination and knew how to dress. He can't be much of a farmer, I thought to myself. How wrong I was!

He created an immediate impression: there was a warmth of personality about him, and he wasn't in the least bit shy. He was very open. Of course, I didn't know at the time where their courtship would lead to. Rhian was very young – only 18 and at college in Bangor, and he was only 20, 18 months older than Rhian.

I later moved to Upper Bangor, to a house called Noddfa in the Crescent, a most convenient house for a gang of lads. He and his friends used to come by often on a Saturday night after being out on the town, and they would stay overnight. He once came with his shirt torn and a cut on his face – a friend of his wanting to fight!

He was a trickster! Once Rhian wanted a new dress to go to the Octagon when she was Miss Bangor having, by the way, also been Miss Anglesey. I saw a dress which would suit her perfectly in a charity shop, a black crocheted dress showing everything underneath because it had big holes in it. I put it on to see how it looked and would it fit. When Gareth saw me in the dress he pushed me through the front door and out into the street, and who happened to be passing but Dilys Jones, a very special lady, and the senior elder of Twrgwyn Chapel at the time. She had such a shock and could only say, 'O Elisabeth!', whilst I prayed for the ground to swallow me up.

Rhian stayed in college for a year. She didn't like the course, and she saw a post being advertised in the advertising department of the *Western Mail*. She applied for it and got it, and there she stayed for two years. Then the newspaper decided to move its office to Cardiff and Gareth didn't think much of the idea of Rhian being in Cardiff. So she gave up her post. Love was more important than a job! And she married into the only family in Wales, as far as I know, where four brothers are still together farming, with their four sons, as one concern.

* * *

To be taken home by your girlfriend's parents is hardly the best way to begin a relationship, but it must have worked because it has lasted. Nevertheless, we met the following evening without her parents, in the Antelope by the Menai Bridge. It was March 1987 and it's over 25 years ago now, but I still love her as much now as I did the first time we met. As well as being lovers we are also friends, and maybe that is the secret.

We quarrel like cats and dogs at times, because I'm an obstinate so-and-so, but I reckon we are a good partnership. She flares up like a match and then forgets about it, whilst I sulk for a couple of days. I work on the farm while she stays at home looking after the children. We decided when our children were born that she would stay at home to bring them up, and that we would live on less in order to bring them up properly. I could not have done half as much as I have in life without Rhian. Life is hard on a farm, and because I do so much with the media also, time is scarce and the days are full.

We lived together in Ty'n Llwyfan before we were married and our first son was born in 1998. Then we decided to get married, in Horeb Chapel, Llanfairfechan, in August 1999, with the wedding reception in Split Willow Hotel in the town. Many of our friends have experienced broken marriages and I think it's a shame for the children when this happens. It is they that suffer most and I wouldn't like to see my children going through such an experience.

Rhian's opinions are very important to me, but I wonder what she'll say about me?

Me through Rhian's eyes

I fell head over heels in love with Gareth the first time I saw him, and I would think about him every night. We were courting for six years before I moved in with him to Ty'n Llwyfan, as it was before being renovated.

I had no idea of the kind of life I would experience after moving in. Gareth had been busily occupied every spare minute redecorating the house, and I would help him especially at weekends. And it was no easy task. In one room we had to strip 15 layers of wallpaper!

I realised very soon that life was hard on a hill farm on the slopes of the Carneddau, very different to a farm on the lowlands of Anglesey. But Gareth never brought his work or his farming problems home with him, and he is still like that. And I have learnt not to ask him anything when he is tired, and he does get tired, believe me.

I had to get acquainted with the rhythm of farming life and realise that regular meal times were important. Gareth prepares his own breakfast, and then there is lunch at twelve and supper at half past five.

I feel safe with Gareth, and his opinion is always wise and emphatic. The paperwork is very complicated but I never do any of it – not that there are any secrets, because it is a family business, but I do not interfere, apart from the time when I had to teach him how to use a computer.

Gareth is well known, if not famous, in many walks of life by now, and maybe many people believe that he is always drawing attention to himself. But he doesn't. I can state with my hand on my heart that he never seeks prominence, but he feels so strongly about things that he must always voice his opinions. He believes that we as Welsh people are reluctant to say what is on our minds, and that we let everything and everyone walk all over us. He won't do that – he'll voice his opinions honestly, without rancour. He'll say what others are often too timid to say. He never feels sorry for saying something but he often feels sorry if he misses the opportunity.

Gareth spends as much time as he can with the children, but life is so busy that I couldn't go out to work if I wanted to. All I can do is lighten his load and turn to the piano and music for relief when I have a minute to spare. Gardening is also therapeutic. I really enjoy working in the garden, with vegetables and flowers.

It is probably an old-fashioned idea, as much of our farming is old-fashioned, but I believe that women who have two jobs – for a salary, and at home – can often lead to broken marriages and divorce. I, like Gareth, strongly believe in giving the children stability.

4

The Children

I AM A softie at heart, although some people get the wrong impression of me, thinking that I'm a hard man because I speak my mind. But being the father of three children has proved to me time and time again that, underneath all the loud-sounding words and opinions voiced with conviction, I am hopelessly sentimental and easily touched. Here are three examples to prove it – one with each child in order to be fair to everyone.

Siôr

Siôr, our eldest son was two years old and playing in the house when he ran into a room where a drawer had been left open. He tripped and fell, catching his face on the corner of the drawer – his two front teeth ended up being bent over backwards and lying flat against the top of his mouth.

The poor lad was crying and shouting and bawling at the top of his voice! He must have been in great pain and he looked for all the world as if someone had struck him in the face with a hammer. There was only one thing for it: to Ysbyty Gwynedd without delay, myself and Rhian with him. We got through the preliminaries fairly quickly and Siôr had quietened down by then, although normal breathing was an effort because he suffered with asthma. The nurse was Welsh and she told us that a doctor would be along in about ten minutes.

When the doctor arrived, an Indian gentleman with a long

beard and a turban on his head, Siôr got the fright of his life and started bawling again. He had never seen anything like it before and when the doctor tried to approach him he struggled and shouted and wouldn't let him touch him. Judging by his reaction, seeing the doctor was a more frightening experience for Siôr than knocking his head against the drawer.

The nurse immediately said that she would get another doctor and the next one who came was an Italian, a pleasant looking young man, and he saw at once that the boy had panicked. He realised that he wouldn't be allowed to touch him, and so he told me that he wanted me to put my finger in his mouth and pull the teeth back into place.

When I heard this I almost fainted and had to quickly grab a chair. Rhian was no better, looking as white as a sheet. But it had to be done, even though my legs were shaking. I only had to move two teeth back to their proper position; nobody was asking me to take his appendix out for goodness sake! But I almost refused.

Rhian eventually got hold of him and I put my finger in his mouth. I thought that the teeth would move easily. However, they were fixed as sound as a bell, and it was with great difficulty that I managed to get them back in place. Somehow, between us, we managed it and they were fine afterwards. They were milk teeth, of course, but losing them could have affected his second teeth.

Siôr was as right as rain after that, but I wasn't. I hope I never have such an experience again. I can do anything to an animal, be it a dog, a sheep or a cow, but my own children? It's a different story then. Hard man? Hardly!

Siôr is now 15 and a pupil at Ysgol Tryfan, Bangor.

Siôr's opinion of me (when he was 12)

Dad is a very serious man and also very funny. He has a lot of humour and life is exciting when he is at home. He is fun to be with and life is never boring. He used to play a lot with us when we were little. He'll get mad at us for a minute and then everything's over. It is impossible to say 'no' to him.

Sometimes he is away for days and it's odd without him, and so I look forward to his coming home. It's all right for a couple of days, but after that I miss him. He sets work for me to do while he's away and I have to complete it before he returns home. But that is no problem.

I receive a little bit of stick from other children at school when he's been on television, but nothing much, and it doesn't worry me in the least. I am proud of my father and of everything he does. I feel safe with him and if there's a problem he will deal with it. He doesn't spoil me but he gives me money when I need it. He loves farming, and so do I. Although farming is a seven days a week occupation and that every day of the year, he has proved to me that it is a good life. Our family have been here for 300 years, and I'm happy to think that I, one day, will be keeping this tradition alive.

Looking back I have to admit that the problem with Siôr's teeth wasn't really a crisis at all, it only appeared to be so at the time. But our experience with Rolant was completely different, a horrible experience, and all of it happening far away from home, which always makes matters worse.

Rolant

It being Halloween and Rhian's birthday, we decided one year to book three days of holiday at Disneyland Paris, leaving on the Thursday and returning on Sunday. On the following Monday I was due to start filming with Griff Rhys Jones for his programme, *Mountain*.

We drove to Liverpool, flew to Paris and were then taken by bus to the hotel. It was a splendid hotel and the children were overjoyed because there was plenty there for them to do. Everything was going well.

To be honest, it wasn't much of a holiday for Rhian and me because the children were small, with Mari still in her pushchair, because walking for a whole day would be too much for her. I was in charge of the pushchair on Halloween when we went to Disneyland on a dark, damp, dismal day. But we had a good time there, going on every ride in the place, but because this was a tiring job I decided, it being Rhian's birthday and all, that we would book dinner in one of the expensive restaurants, Planet Hollywood.

We had an excellent meal, enjoyed ourselves enormously with everyone getting whatever they wanted. On the way out we saw this huge wall and on it were the hand imprints of famous people who had visited the place. So we spent a few minutes looking at the names, people like Clint Eastwood, Sylvester Stallone and many of the Hollywood stars were there and the children were quite excited.

Suddenly I realised that Rolant wasn't with us. 'Where is Rolant?' I asked looking around for him, but he was nowhere to be seen. Rolant is the kind of child who would never leave you, like a dog at your heels all the time. Had Siôr or Mari disappeared I wouldn't have been so surprised, but Rolant? Never. Always by your side, often clutching your hand, needing security, especially in a crowd.

It was eight o'clock, a dark night with lights everywhere. People were milling around like ants, with all sorts of characters dressed up in colourful clothes and some walking on stilts. It would be so easy for someone to kidnap a child. And I, a farmer from the hills of the Carneddau, was in strange unfamiliar surroundings, like a fish out of water. I panicked. Completely!

'Someone has taken him,' I said to Rhian. 'You stay here whilst I get the security people.' And off I went to the main entrance.

Two men in yellow jackets were there by the gate talking to a third person, and I rushed up to them. But they had very little English, and I tried to tell them that someone had taken my child and that they had to close the gates.

'You're in luck,' said the third person, 'I am head of security.'

His English was perfect. 'Now, calm down,' he said. 'When did you lose him?'

'A few minutes ago,' I said. 'And I know that he would never leave my side of his own free will. Someone must have taken him.'

'Let me tell you something,' he said in an effort to calm me down. 'We get half a dozen cases like this every day, and all that has happened is that children have wandered away from their families and got lost.' And then his first question: 'What was he wearing?'

I couldn't for the life of me remember what he had on. I can usually control myself pretty well, but it was as if my brain had frozen over. He said something to the other two and I yelled: 'Close the bloody gates!'

'We can't do that,' he said. 'Come, we'll go back to where you were when you realised that he was missing, and start from there.'

We got back to the others and, of course, Rhian knew exactly what he was wearing. I have to admit she was much calmer than I was.

The security man then told me to stay where I was.

'No chance,' I replied, 'I'm going to look for him.'

'You'll never find him,' he said, 'He's just got lost and *we'll* find him.'

Funnily enough, the main thought going through my mind was that I would have to return home without him, and that I would have to explain to my mother and father that I had lost him. That was really the least of my worries, but everything was a muddle in my head and my brain wasn't functioning properly. I have never had such an experience before or since. I decided to go along the main thoroughfare and try to imagine, if someone had snatched him, where they would take him – down some dark path or avenue probably.

I was like a man possessed, struggling against the constant tide of people going in the opposite direction – some dressed as pumpkins, knocking everyone on the head with rubber batons;

many on stilts, everybody moving and laughing, with noise and music filling the air. And me like a wild bull rushing ahead not knowing exactly what I was doing, looking in vain for Rolant, down one or two dark passages, round the back of some of the buildings, on and on for almost an hour, which seemed like an eternity with the anxiety and sorrow choking me. But there was no sign of Rolant, and to my mind, as time went on the hope of finding him was rapidly disappearing.

At long last, after looking everywhere and having gone down every path and passage, I approached the end of the street where the crowd was thinner, and I saw two security men, one a big black man and the other smaller, both smoking. And I went to them. 'I've lost my son,' I said over and over. They hadn't much English but they understood something and asked a question. 'Rolant,' I said, and I must have given the correct answer because he reached for his phone and started talking to someone, saying 'oui, oui' every now and again. 'Good,' he said, or something akin to that, and switched off his phone. 'We found him,' he said.

I immediately embraced the man and he was shocked by my reaction, and the other one started laughing. But it was such a feeling... well I have never felt anything like it. 'Go, go,' he said, and I returned to where Rhian and the other two children were, rushing through the crowd like a maniac, but it was easier this time because I was going with the flow.

And there was Rolant looking as calm as you like, standing with a security man, and I just grabbed him. Every time the feeling I had then returns, my eyes fill with tears.

As we were coming out of the restaurant he had followed a woman who was wearing similar clothes to Rhian, thinking that she was his mother. He had followed her across the street and into a large building, a kind of superstore selling toys, and he had been walking up and down looking at this and that. He hadn't panicked at all – quite different to his father!

One of the staff in the shop noticed him and realised that he was on his own and she went to him and asked him his name.

Then, of course, the whole security system was set in motion and every security person got his name.

For three-quarters of an hour or more I had been in utter panic, and the feeling of relief I had afterwards was unbelievable. I had been to both extremes of emotion, and the swing from one to the other made me feel totally confused. I didn't let him out of my sight for the rest of the time; indeed I don't believe I let go of him until we arrived back at the hotel.

The following day we were returning home and, as if losing Rolant wasn't enough of a trauma, we were driven to the wrong airport, my needing to be back home in time to take part in the programme, *Mountain*. We had scarcely an hour to rush from one airport to the other, and it cost me €50, which was money down the drain – because we were too late to board the plane.

There were harsh words between me and the person who refused to let us to get on the plane, although there were 20 minutes before take off time. I wasn't my usual self after the trauma of the previous day, but Rhian managed to cool things down, thank goodness, and the official told us that we would be allowed on the next plane. But that would not be for another twelve hours, and we stayed at the airport the whole time. It cost me a fortune. I have never been to such an expensive place and the children were demanding something all the time!

The researcher from *Mountain* phoned about a dozen times whilst we were at the airport, but there was nothing we could do. However, all's well that ends well, we were home in time for the filming, having spent all our money and more, but all members of the family were safe and that was the important thing. It could have been so different and I've had many a nightmare since thinking about it.

Me through Rolant's eyes (when he was 10)

Dad is a busy, hard working, nice, kind man. He is never really cross with me but I sometimes get a telling off when I've not tidied my bedroom. I like it when other children tell me that they have seen him on television or heard him on the radio – I feel proud of him then.

When he goes away I feel quite sad, especially if he's away for days on end. If he's left me some work to do he praises me for doing it when he gets home. Usually, my work on the farm is to help Dad and Siôr, carry logs and close the hens and geese for the night. Siôr owns the hens and I own the ducks.

He was really frightened when I got lost in Eurodisney, but neither he nor Mam scolded me, because they were so glad to find me. I like living on the farm, but I don't want to be a farmer when I grow up, unlike Siôr.

Thinking back, the problem with Siôr's teeth was nothing compared to the other experiences, and the Eurodisney experience was an uncalled-for anxiety, more or less self-induced, but we nearly lost Mari Non a fortnight after she was born. Thank goodness, she's now ten years old going on 21!

Mari Non

Rhian and I didn't want to know beforehand whether we were going to have another boy, or a girl, although a scan would have told us. But I was convinced that it would be a girl. Expressing hope, perhaps, because we had two boys and it would be nice to have a girl. An experienced midwife was looking after Rhian before the birth, an awkward old cuss, and after the birth she was no better. She had behaved exactly the same before Siôr's birth, and there had been a problem then because he was a breech baby and she was of no help at all.

However, we spent a day in hospital when Rhian gave birth to Mari Non, and then we came home and Rhian was breast-feeding as she had with the other two. Mari had diarrhoea from the start and she was very sore. The midwife maintained that it was Rhian's fault, although she was very careful about what she ate.

But Mari was getting no better and, after eleven days, when Rhian gave her her first bath, her navel fell off and she was badly infected underneath. She was so sore that night that she started bleeding. Rhian took her to see the doctor and he gave her some ointment but things got no better. She would not settle, and we thought that it was indigestion. But things went from bad to worse – she developed a high temperature and Rhian took her back to the doctor's. After taking one look at her and taking her temperature, he told Rhian to take her to Bangor immediately, and in the meantime he would call the hospital to tell them that she was on her way. Rhian asked if she could go home first to collect some things, but the answer was 'no'. It was a case of hospital immediately.

When they arrived at the hospital, Mari was taken away from Rhian and she phoned me at once. It was a busy time on the farm, time to round up the sheep for shearing, but I received help from kind neighbours and got to Bangor in a hurry. It only took me ten minutes that day.

I insisted on going to the room where Mari was, and there I found a doctor trying to push a needle into the back of her hand in order to feed her blood with antibiotics. Mari was screaming as the doctor bent her hand. I can't hide my feelings, I've got to say what's on my mind, and I told the nurse in Welsh that the doctor was not to touch Mari or I would create a scene. I didn't have to. Another nurse, a kind Welsh one, came to put the needle successfully in her hand, in two places. Mari was in a bad way, she had septicaemia and it could have killed her. It was touch and go, but thank heavens, they got her in time and she and Rhian spent many days in the hospital, in an out of the day room because MRSA was present there at the time.

It was a very anxious time for us – another couple of days and it would have been too late because a baby doesn't have an immune system to cope and any infection goes immediately into the blood stream.

And when we hear of families losing little babies, we can

imagine how they feel because we came so near to losing ours.

Me through the eyes of Mari Non (when she was six)

Dad works hard and shouts a bit if we are naughty, fighting and things like that. Sometimes I get the blame when it's not my fault. And he steals my chocolate. When Mam has bought me Crunchy Pudding, he goes into the fridge and steals it.

Sometimes other children say that Dad is weird, and that he is not famous. It's boys who say that, not my friends.

I like Dad, he's a tough cookie. Once he was accidentally struck on the head with an axe, but he didn't cry out.

He is very clever and very strong, he can carry eight logs at a time, and he is fast too, faster than me when he runs. Sometimes he doesn't let me go with him to sheepdog trials nor does he let me work with him when it's dangerous. He is good with dogs and trains my little dog.

And that's quite enough about the Joneses for the time being.

5

The Carneddau

Looming over the farms and casting its shadow over all the inhabitants of the area, including our family and company members, is the Carneddau, the vast expanse of mountainous area stretching from Bethesda and the A5 in the west and south, to the Conwy valley in the east, and northwards almost to the coastline. As well as thousands of acres of desolate plateau, moorland, lakes and streams, stone walls and sheep folds, it comprises of 19 peaks, six of them around 1,000 metres (over 3,000 feet) and the highest Carnedd Llewelyn (1,064m) is only 21m lower than Snowdon, and two others, Carnedd Dafydd and Pen yr Ole Wen, are slightly lower still.

The Carneddau are wonderful in summer, a medley of green and purple patterns attracting tourists to walk along its paths and the old Roman road, to gaze in wonder at the views and to see nature at its best.

But in winter it changes its character completely, becoming bare and severe, and unwelcoming, and it is a hard struggle for man and beast to survive in such a place.

My farm, Ty'n Llwyfan, as is true of all the other farms in the area, consists of three parts – the lower land, the moorland, and the mountain which is Crown land. And on the mountain are the ponies – the famous Carneddau ponies – a small, tough breed that was first introduced, according to history, by the Romans and then developed by the Celts before those tribes were even called Welsh. These animals have survived every threat to their existence, including Henry VIII's order to kill every animal under twelve hands because they were too small to be war horses.

Our family's connection with the ponies dates back at least 300 years and my great-grandfather used to sell some of them to the coal mines. They were ideal for work in the coal tunnels as they were small but sturdy, with strong bones and a capacity for hard work.

They never leave the mountain, except when we round them up and bring them down to treat them and trim their tails. Even during the toughest of winters they remain on the mountain. Dad remembers, during the terrible winter of 1947 when he was eight years old, going with the men to take some hay up to the ponies, and the ponies refusing to eat, as they weren't used to it. They would rather starve than eat something that was foreign to them, and they would rather freeze in their habitat than come down from the mountain. Dad saw a pony and her foal frozen to death that winter and still standing upright.

The ponies are not the property of the company, but are owned by Dad and Uncle Teg. Their brand mark is the letter 'O', after my grandfather, Owen Jones, and they inherited the ponies from him. Not all the ponies belong to members of our family, of course; other farmers have grazing and pony rights on the mountain, and each farm has its own brand mark for the ponies. It's a big day when we all come together to round them up and bring them down from the mountain to be treated. The quad bikes roar and Griff Rhys Jones, the well-known TV celebrity, compared the cacophony of sound to hearing a recording of Rommel's tanks attacking in the Second World War.

They are wild animals, of course, and they must be tamed before they can become useful. Dad has tamed a pony for each of my children, as he did for my brother and me when we were small. But children soon grow too big for them.

The ponies have caused quite a bit of hassle for our family, have survived a few crises and have brought some income to both the owners as well. At one time the money came from

Me about 16 months old

Black-leading with Tamzin

Do I look full of mischief? Clive, me and Huw Bach, my brother

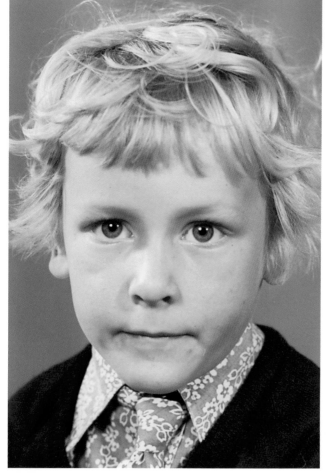

Ready to go to school in my flowery tie

Me and Huw Bach

Punk rockers at Llanfairfechan
Carnival: Aled Lewis, Huw, my
cousin Rich, and me

Me, about 11 years old, with my cousin Rich

Me as an 11 year old

On a trip to Ireland with my mates

After winning my first cup with Spot, at Aber and Llanfairfechan dog races

With my cousin Robat

At Llanfairfechan dog races: Julie and Audrey Lovell-Smith, Berwyn, Heulwen, Huw bach, Richard and me

Me, Huw and Keith

Glynllifon College: Back row from the left: Ems, me, John bach, Glyn. Front row: Edward Tremogoch, Robin Trebedda, Paul Bach, Gethin

With the ponies on the farmyard; Uncle Wil, Dad, me, and my cousin Ieuan (1986)

With which one of these did I fall in love? Caroline, 10; Catherine, 8; Rhian, 5 (1975)

I've been courting Rhian
for a week

Corfu – Rhian and me (1987)

'Fancy man'
Mrs Robinson

Attending to the Christmas turkeys with Dad

'I'm too sexy for this farm!'

Rhian (1987)

Rhian with her mother when
they lived in Upper Bangor

Rounding up the ponies with Dad (1988)

On the slope of Dinas with my dog, Beti (1990)

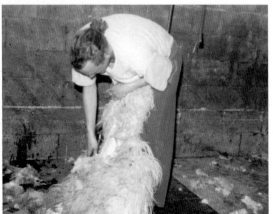

My hair was long, so it had to be tied back for shearing (1992)

With Rhian at
Abergwyngregyn falls
(1990)

I wonder if
Steve is still
under that
bonnet?

'Puss, puss!'

Astride a bike on Zante

Catching fish in Miami

Pretty boys! Mark and me in Miami. Mark had found a small toad with red eyes!

On holiday in Kos

Back-breaking work with my pick and shovel

Marriage (1999)

Our first dance. 'You're the one that I want – ooh, ooh, ooh, honey!'

Pesda Roc. From the left: Steven, Catherine, Gary, Caroline, Rhian and me

From the left: Mum and Dad, Auntie Sandra and Uncle Teg, Auntie Iris and Uncle Wil, Auntie Ann and Uncle Huw, Auntie Rhianwen and Uncle Bobi

Rounding up the ponies. Enough to scare Griff Rhys Jones! Ieuan, Uncle Teg, Wil Gwyndy, Robat, me, Mark Hughes, Myrfyn Parry, Dad, Ken Gwyndy, Berwyn, Robat Owen and Uncle Wil

About to attend to the ponies: Robat, Marc Ginger (in the background), Mair, Dad, Geraint, Uncle Teg and me

The five brothers, from the youngest to the eldest: Teg, Rol (Dad), Wil, Huw and Bobi

Dad and Mun

the National Park and the Countryside Commission, but today it comes from the Assembly Government through Natural Resources Wales, and there is a particular reason why we receive this money.

Years ago, pony market prices were extremely low, and they were worth next to nothing. Dad took twelve of them to the sale in Bryncir and had to bring ten back after selling two for such a low price that he might as well have given them away for free.

At that time a newspaper reporter came here to enquire about the ponies in order to write an article about them. Dad told him that he would have to get rid of them if market prices didn't improve. What he meant, of course, was that he would have to sell them for a low price, but the reporter retorted by saying that he wouldn't be able to get rid of them all as some would not be found, the mountainous area being so vast. 'Well,' Dad said as a joke, 'if there are any left and I find them, I'll shoot them.'

The following week there appeared a big heading in the local paper: 'All Carneddau ponies to be shot.'

Almost as soon as the newspaper came off the presses there was a frantic phone call for Dad from Rhys Owen, one of the National Park's officers, asking if the story in the paper was true.

'I never lie,' Dad said to him. 'But what I said was that I'd sell them, not shoot them. I've entered them into the Morgan Evans sale next week.'

Rhys Owen was shocked when he heard this and asked my father to hold on to them until he had spoken to someone in authority in Cardiff. The result was that Uncle Teg and Dad were offered money to look after the ponies and towards the cost of managing, treating, sorting them, before selling a limited number annually. Part of the money was also used to pay for legal costs when establishing The Carneddau Pony Society. Another condition tied to the money was that they weren't to be given any medicine to treat worms.

The obvious question is why the National Park and the Countryside Commission, and nowadays the Assembly Government through Natural Resources Wales, were so keen to protect these ponies and pay money for their maintenance and well-being. The answer is simple – the chough, the red-legged black birds that live on the Carneddau. The worms in the ponies' dung are an important part of their diet. If there were no worms, there would be no choughs on the mountain. Indeed, the Countryside Commission and the National Park buy some of the Carneddau ponies to put them in habitats in other areas of the country to develop and protect the chough.

The worms aren't the only elements in the ponies' importance regarding the chough's existence. Ponies graze differently to sheep, they graze much closer to the ground, and this makes it easier for the chough to search the soil for insects.

Low market prices weren't the only thing that threatened the ponies. European Common Market policies were also a threat, because ear marking was made illegal and had to be replaced by a chip place under the nape of each pony. In my opinion this rule was instigated by bureaucrats who know nothing of life in such a habitat as the Carneddau, wrongly assuming that ear marks are cruel and not realising the hassle and cost of putting a chip in each pony, something that is totally unsuitable for the ponies and for the mountain as well.

The ponies are on the mountain throughout the winter, but the sheep are not. At least they aren't supposed to be there and the authorities employ someone in each parish, which has part of the mountain within its boundaries, to be a settler, a person who ensures that the area is completely cleared of sheep, and settles any dispute regarding rights, dealing with the stray sheep and resolving disputes between farmers.

Dad has been appointed this parish's settler and he has to go up the mountain often during the summer and winter. As part of the agreement between the authority and the farmers who graze the mountain, no sheep are allowed there between the end of October and the first of April and part of Dad's job is to make sure this rule is adhered to.

The arrangement works well. We receive a payment for bringing the sheep down from the mountain, and the sheep thrive much more from spending six months on lower land during the winter. As a result, the sheep and lambs are stronger, and the wool and meat is of a better standard. Years ago we would move the sheep to other farms for wintering on the lowlands, but that arrangement has come to an end as we have enough land of our own, owned or rented. The reason why Natural Resources Wales doesn't want the sheep on the mountain during the winter is to protect the land for the ponies and give it time to recover. Pony grazing isn't as destructive as sheep grazing.

Comprising ten per cent of the whole of Snowdonia, the Carneddau is a substantial part of Wales, and one of the people who was absolutely enthralled with the place was Griff Rhys Jones. He came here in 2006 to film for his series of programmes, *Mountain*. He came to witness the rounding of the ponies and he was astonished to see the large numbers of us that were preparing for the task, from our company and from other farms that have ponies on the Carneddau. He was also surprised that we all spoke Welsh, and had a lot of fun with plenty of bantering and leg-pulling going on. Some people can be so ignorant, even of aspects of the country they were born in! One of the first lessons that he learnt was how to pronounce his own name, Rhys, because he called himself 'Reece', and the assembled gathering wouldn't have that.

The bikes had quite an impact on him as well, and he travelled up the mountain on the back of mine, holding on for dear life and complaining that his bum was being bounced ruthlessly. This is how he describes the beginning of the journey:

Sixteen or so red-faced farmers, their sons, their uncles and their cousins, in a variety of woolly hats and mounted on a fearsome armada of fat-tyred, mud-spattered quad bikes began revving their two-stroke engines in chorus. It was the Wild Welsh Bunch. The noise was incredible. The bikes were battered and grungy.

Griff Rhys Jones, *Mountain*

All the way up and after we had arrived beyond the mountain wall, I tried to explain to him what was happening – quite a challenge because of the roar of the bikes and the fact that the wind snatched the words from my mouth. But, despite the uncomfortable ride, he loved it and had a day to remember, a day in which he got an opportunity to learn about what happens in a rounding operation of this kind and why it happens at all. The views also astonished him, and he saw them at their best because it was a clear summer's day. He had a wonderful experience, but not of the mountain ferociously showing its teeth. It's a totally different place then, and we have to cope with the mountain no matter its mood.

I remember the time when sheep were on the mountain all through the winter and remember the effort made to look after them in bad weather. Being on the mountain during that time taught me a lot. I remember the winter of 1987 when a few of us had to go up in the snow. Keith, who worked with Yncl Teg and who was like an older brother to me, and myself were in our early twenties and we were quite cocky and thought we knew the lot and could cope with anything. With us was Wil Tyddyn Angharad, a man who was in his 60s and enjoyed his whisky, but who had been with the Special Forces during the war and was surprisingly fit.

We went on our bikes as far as the mountain wall but couldn't ride them any further. We had to walk.

'Come on,' Keith said to me, 'we'll go on, and let the old people catch up with us.'

So off we went with the dogs through the deepening snow, and before too long we were exhausted and struggling. Who came past us with a strong smell of whisky on his breath but Wil, together with his five dogs, dogs that were like wolves, and by the time we had reached the first batch of sheep he was already rounding them up. He didn't need to say anything – he had taught us young lads a lesson, we who thought that we could do everything and knew the lot!

Everything regarding the Carneddau works well for us now, but that wasn't always the case. The matter of keeping to the *Cynefin*[1] – hefting as it is called – has been complicated, especially the issue of grazing rights on parts of the mountain that belong to particular farm flocks. When the sheep were on the mountain, more or less throughout the year, giving birth to their lambs, there they knew their heft and would keep quite close to it, but one thing that conflicted against this was the weather causing problems, a problem that once led to a court case for Dad and his two brothers.

The farmers who grazed a part of the mountain above Abergwyngregyn (Aber to the local people) didn't accept the fact that our company had the right to graze there and yet, during windy weather, when the wind was blowing from a particular direction, our sheep, around 500 of them, would wander to the mountain above Aber where there was more shelter and where they had every right to be.

But this is not how the farmers of Aber saw things and Dad and his brothers had to go to a civil court in Caernarfon to argue over Owen Jones's hefting rights on that part of the mountain. It had developed into a nasty situation that only a court of law could resolve, but our company won, and it was proved that Aber's sheep also wandered over to our heft when the wind blew from the other direction. All of this is behind us now; it is all ancient history, thank goodness for that. We have been one community of grazers for years and get along well. The chairman is my cousin Tudor, and my second cousin, Liam Jones, is the secretary and I'm the treasurer.

---

1   Cynefin: a part of a mountain that is the habitat of sheep from a particular farm – sheep that are on the mountain throughout the year keep to their habitat without need of a fence to keep them within it.

If that problem has long been resolved by now, another problem has arisen due to the fact that the sheep aren't on the mountain all the year round. We have no right to put them there between October and April, so they are less certain of their heft. When they go back up at the beginning of April, it's not enough to leave them once they have been driven beyond the mountain wall; we must take them to where they are supposed to be. We have to establish the heft, and by doing that there is every chance that they will stay within their back-yard.

From our point of view, all human problems having been resolved, there remains only the weather storms to cause disturbance on the mountain now. There is, for us farmers who have grazing rights there, in the words of Ieuan Wyn,[2] *'hedd ar y Carneddau'* (peace on the Carneddau).

---

2   Ieuan Wyn is a well-known Welsh poet who has won the chair at the National Eisteddfod. He lives in Bethesda, another village nestling in the shadow of the Carneddau.

6

Facing Justice

SHEEP AND THEIR hefting was the reason Dad had to appear in a civil court of law. I, however, found myself in a Crown Court, because of cattle, not sheep, an example of one-upmanship I could easily have done without!

Selling two bullocks in Gaerwen market, Anglesey, through Morgan Evans's auctioneering company, on two separate occasions and after completing all the necessary paperwork, were such normal acts that no one, not even a person with the clearest insight could have foreseen that they would result in a protracted criminal case brought against me. This a case dragged on for over two years, ending with an interesting footnote as recently as 2009!

The first bullock was sold on 13 August 2004 – I have the details in front of me right now – to S.L. Morgan. Then, on 8 October in the same year, the other bullock was sold to Monk Bros, one of north Wales's biggest dealers.

The necessary paperwork referred to includes a passport with details of lineage, age and so on and, as usual, I carefully followed all guidelines – these had greatly increased following the crisis brought about by mad cow disease. The bullocks were two years old, sold as store cattle to be fattened for a few weeks before being slaughtered for their meat. I've never had any trouble in matters like these, and once the work is done and the animals are sold, that's the end of the matter.

But not this time. In November I received a copy of a letter sent to the Monk Brothers by Zoë Lewis, an Animal Health

Officer from Merthyr Tydfil County Borough Council's Trading Standards Department, dated 11 November 2004, a letter that gave me quite a shock. This is what it said:

Concerning: Trade Descriptions Act Animal Recognition Regulations 1989

On Sunday, 31 October 2004, you supplied St Merryn Meat Ltd, Merthyr Tydfil with an animal (numbered). A portmortem examination has revealed that the animal had six teeth.

I am writing to inform you that further enquiries are being conducted and that an offence under the above regulations may have been committed.

I shall be in touch with you again regarding this matter.

You who are farmers will understand immediately what the problem was. The animal had been sold in Gaerwen as a two-year-old bullock, and I would swear that it was. I would never be dishonest and fiddle with the age of animals. You would always be found out in any case because every animal is examined before being slaughtered. But when this particular bullock was killed it had six teeth, which would make it a two-and-a-half to three-year-old animal.

It had to be binned because it was too old to enter the food chain, and before the end of the year I received a bill from the Morgan Evans company for the price I got for the bullock and an extra £117 for getting rid of it. I reluctantly paid the bill in January 2005 thinking that it would be the end of the matter, but there was worse to come.

I received a phone call from Zoë Lewis, the one who had sent the letter to Monk Bros, a woman who sounded a right old bitch, saying she wanted to come to see me as it was possible that fraud had been committed, either by Monk Bros or by me. We arranged for her to come to the farm and, after introducing herself, the first thing she did was give me a formal warning that everything was being recorded and that anything I said could be used in evidence against me in court.

I had no objection whatsoever to her recording the interview because I honestly believed that the cattle were of the correct age and therefore that I had done nothing wrong. I told her that I had never been in any trouble and that I always tried to be as honest as possible. Maybe that was my mistake. I should have kept quiet, only answering the questions she asked me. She said she was going to interview G.R. and S.J. Monk as well, and that she had concrete evidence that the animal's age was two-and-a-half years.

I was really beginning to wonder whether we were talking about the same bullock or not, but then she said we could give the mother a blood test to establish the true facts.

Before the end of February, following her visit, I received another letter from her informing me that she'd been looking into the records of two animals that had been reared on the farm. Yes, it was two by now; the one sold to Monk Bros and the one sold to S.L. Morgan. She noted in the letter that both animals had six teeth and were possibly over two and a half years old. We then had to arrange for someone to come to the farm to give both mothers a blood test. This was done, but the results were inconclusive.

Following this the letters started coming, one after the other, including a letter informing me that I would have to appear in court accused of fraud, as an individual, rather than as the company's secretary: 'Trading standards vs. yourself' as the letter noted. I was told that according to specialist advice, the animals had six teeth and were much older than I had stated, between two and a half and three years old.

It had now become a legal matter, and our solicitors were J.W. Hughes and Sons, Conwy. I was told that I would receive legal aid and would incur no personal cost when defending myself in the magistrates' court. I was informed that Monk Bros and S.L. Morgan would also be defendants, but the case against the latter was postponed due to ill health, but not the accusations against me for selling him an animal that was too old to enter the food chain.

As Merthyr Tydfil was four hours drive away, it was agreed

that a video link could be arranged from the court in Llandudno. The case was conducted on 23 November 2005 – more than a year after I had sold the animals! But the three magistrates refused to discuss the matter because they considered it to be too serious for a magistrates' court, so it was transferred at once to the Crown Court.

It really was a most serious matter by now. I needed a barrister, not a solicitor, and their fees can be more than £400 an hour. Legal aid was only available for the magistrates' court. But I was lucky, the company rent Plas Newydd, the Marquis's farm, and his land agent is Trefor Lloyd, who is also a barrister in Chester. He told us he knew the very man to help us with our problem, Simon Rogers, the son of Peter Rogers who was once an Assembly candidate for Anglesey.

We arranged to go to Chester for a meeting, and when I drove into the car park I realised that every car there was worth more than £50,000! The building was also impressive. We met Trefor Lloyd who introduced me to Simon Rogers. I told him things from my perspective, that I did all the paperwork for the business and that I thought everything was within the rules and that the animals were under 30 months old. By today, it would have made no difference, but in those days selling an animal over 30 months old to be killed was an offence, and that was the accusation against me.

It was agreed that Simon Rogers would be my barrister, and there followed the exchange of many letters between us. As the case was to be heard in a Crown Court, the lawyers had to give an estimate of the likely cost if I contested the accusation. In a letter dated 25 November 2005 I was told the cost would be between £450 and £550 if I pleaded guilty, but if I pleaded not guilty I had to consider costs of at least £2,000, depending on the length of the trial.

We were informed that the first hearing would be in Merthyr Crown Court on 16 December 2005, and I was asked to supply all the relevant documents for the barristers and also the results of the DNA test on the cattle. These were all forwarded, but the blood didn't match that of the animals killed, which struck me as being very strange. But it meant that the result of the blood test couldn't be used as part of my defence.

The barrister told me that I needed character witnesses and many people from Llanfairfechan agreed to support me. I was grateful for that and felt much better after receiving their written testimonies. It was a very difficult period for me, the case being against me, not the company. To make matters worse, the barrister had told me that a prison sentence was a possible outcome if I was found guilty.

We asked for permission to appear in court in Llandudno, using the video link like before, but Merthyr Crown Court didn't have the necessary facilities. I was also informed that Simon Rogers would be unable to attend the court hearing because another case he was involved with coincided with the hearing at Merthyr. It was arranged that the Jenkins Newman Partnership would act on my behalf and that a barrister from the Merthyr area would represent me in court. Josie Fletcher was the person from the partnership who contacted me, a very pleasant woman, and she arranged for a barrister called Owen Preece-Lewis, a Welshman, to represent me.

I was all set to travel down to Merthyr for the case when I received a phone call and a letter informing me the case had been postponed until 22 December – three days before Christmas – and that I had to be there by half past nine to meet the barrister and a representative from Jenkins Newman Partnership.

So, on the 21st, I drove down to Merthyr. It was almost Christmas and the roads were quiet and I felt quite lonely, my mind being with the family at home: Rhian busy with the preparations and the children looking forward to opening their presents. I stayed at the Castle Hotel in Merthyr and I tried to relax. But there was a Christmas party in the hotel, and it was a very noisy one, so I went out in search of a meal.

As I walked the streets, I was struck by the appearance of the place, with signs of poverty everywhere. I came across a

Wetherspoon pub and had a meal there before going for another walk. I was strolling along one of the back streets when I saw a small pub, and decided to go in for a pint. The place went deadly quiet as I walked in, you could hear a pin drop and everyone was staring at me as if I had horns growing out of my head. I was tempted to turn on my heel and run, because to be honest I was a bit scared. But I conquered my fear and walked up to the bar to order a pint, and I soon realised as I looked around that it was one of the pubs that had appeared on Sky's programme on the world's toughest pubs!

Scars covered the barman's face and the walls and shelves were full of boxing memorabilia. The customers were all hard cases – former boxers, or at least with some boxing connection.

'You're not from round here,' said the barman.

'No,' I answered. Then he asked me what I was doing there, and I decided to be honest in case he sensed I was lying. I think I did the right thing, because when I told him I was in court the following day it seemed that everyone began to respect me a bit more. I didn't tell them why I was in court; I let them think what they liked.

The barman knew who the judge was; in fact I think he and his customers knew a lot about Merthyr's courts! 'He's a tough one,' he told me, just what I needed to hear!

I returned to the Castle and went to bed. The party was in full swing and the sound deafening, but that's not why I failed to sleep a wink that night. I couldn't stop worrying about the morning, and what would happen to me.

Simon Rogers had advised me to plead guilty; to plead guilty even though I knew I was innocent. This played on my mind as I arrived in court the following morning and met the barrister. He had all the documents, including my statement.

He told me the case could cost up to £30,000 if I pleaded not guilty. Indeed, if the case dragged on it could be as much as £100,000. He'd read all the documents and according to him I didn't have a foot to stand on, all the evidence pointed towards my being guilty, even though he knew how convinced I was of my innocence.

'If I were you,' he said, 'I'd plead guilty.'

Yes, the same advice as Simon Rogers had given me.

When I heard this I felt as sick as a parrot, and completely alone, missing the family more than ever. I wanted someone to tell them, and to tell me, that I was doing the right thing. I phoned Dad and told him my dilemma, and the advice I had received.

'Do what you think is best,' he said. 'We'll all be behind you whatever you decide, and the company will pay for everything, whatever the cost.'

It wasn't the money I was worried about, but the idea of a long case and my name being dragged through the mud even though I was innocent.

However, we went into court, expecting a long case that would be postponed over Christmas to restart in January. The lawyer asked me how I pleaded.

'Guilty,' I said. The place went quiet, and I felt great relief that the case was over before it had really begun.

I noticed Zoë Lewis, the Trading Standards woman wearing a big smile on her face. Jeff Monk was also smiling, and I could have choked the little sod! But what I did was smile myself and wink at him, and I felt better because he had no idea how to respond.

The judge said he'd have to consider the sentence and that I would have to appear in court again to hear the outcome of his deliberations.

There followed months of waiting, but after a long series of legal letters going back and forth, I was informed that I would be sentenced by the judge in Merthyr on the 22 May 2006, almost five months after I had pleaded guilty.

I travelled there on the previous day as before, and stayed in the same hotel – but I slept like a log this time.

When I arrived in court I was taken to the box which had reinforced glass around it, walking there between two police officers as if I was a dangerous murderer! It was a horrible feeling, and I could imagine what it would feel like if I had killed someone.

The judge began by saying that he'd read all the documents and that I was clearly a respectable man and a strong member of my community, and that he was hesitant about sentencing me. He gave me the lightest sentence possible. There were four charges, two of selling the animals and two of submitting false passports. I received a fine of £50 for each one, a total of £200. But the court costs were almost £4,000. I wasn't happy that I'd been forced to plead guilty, but I felt I could walk from court with my head held high.

But the story doesn't end there. Monk Bros weren't happy that the sentence was so light, even though I'd pleaded guilty. J.W. Hughes, my lawyers in Conwy, received a letter from their lawyers, Messrs Walker Smith Way of Chester, stating that their client was entitled to compensation for aggravated damages. This was fiercely opposed, but in the end it was agreed that I would pay £500 without prejudice in order to end the matter.

And that was that, thank goodness.

Well, not quite, there was one other twist!

In the *Daily Post*'s farming section on 18 June 2009 there was a report that one of north Wales's main cattle and sheep dealers was facing a court case in Merthyr Tydfil over accusations relating to the tagging of animals. Merthyr Council's Trading Standards Department was taking action in relation to animals sold by Monk Bros to St Merryn Meat slaughterhouse. Do the names: Merthyr Council, St Merryn Meats, and Monk Bros ring a bell? They should!

The animals I had sold had nothing to do with this case because that had taken place three years earlier. But it makes you think, doesn't it? Made me think, anyway.

And there's another footnote to this tale. In the *Daily Post* on 7 July 2009, it was reported that Monk Bros had gone bankrupt. The company had to pay a fine of £750 when it was found guilty of tagging offences, and thousands in legal fees,

but the debt it owed to nine auction companies was shocking –
somewhere in the region of £1.5 million. The newspaper noted
three reasons for the company's troubles:

> It is understood three factors played a role in the firm's collapse: a
> recent court case, a disputed invoice with St Merryn Meat abattoir,
> Llanybydder, and the legacy of last year's bluetongue restrictions.

A sad case for the animal trade in north Wales, but what
came to mind as I read about the case was Nain's words: 'Life
goes around in circles, and what goes around comes around
eventually.' The chickens, more often than not, come home to
roost!

7

Emergencies

WE ALL EXPERIENCE our share of emergencies, but thankfully most of them never lead to a court of law or to someone's death. There are emergencies you can, with hindsight, laugh about, even though they seemed very serious at the time. There are others that raise important questions and those that are a consequence of your own actions. I've experienced all of these during my lifetime, and this chapter tells the story of a few of them.

Cattle

Cattle are domesticated animals, but there are degrees of domesticity and many people know to their cost that they are not pets and that they can be very dangerous at times. And not only bulls. Any cattle farmer will tell you that a cow with a young calf can be much more dangerous. We have about 120 cattle in our sheds, and over a 100 have calves. We know each and every one, and one cow comes to mind immediately – normally a quiet placid animal – but when she has a calf, you can't go anywhere near her for at least three weeks!

Over the years we've had our share of escapades with cattle! Three years ago we were treating some of them at Plas Newydd, Anglesey. We had about a 100 cattle in the shed and Uncle Wil was with us. He was 78 then, and had been in the wars, having had two kneecap replacements, three in fact, because the first one wasn't successful.

We were nearly done, releasing each animal through the gate as we finished with it. There was one heifer amongst the ones left, and she was a bit wild and agitated. As we were trying to release her she escaped into a shed and Uncle Wil went after her. The heifer reared up on her back legs like a horse, and with her two front ones knocked Uncle Wil to the ground, breaking his leg and shoulder. But it could have been even worse. There were concrete girders on the floor of the shed and had he hit his head on one of them, the blow might well have killed him.

Uncle Wil is tough though, and the ambulance only took five minutes to arrive and the paramedics treated him before taking him to hospital. They were very nice lads, and Uncle Wil is perfectly fine now.

A few years earlier we had trouble with a bullock.

Uncle Teg, Dad's youngest brother, had some cattle at Plas Ucha, Penmaenmawr. They were in the fields quite close to the village and the school, and they needed to be moved.

Robat, Ieuan and I went to move them, and we had no trouble with most of them, apart from two bullocks who charged towards us. They were completely wild. There was nothing for it but to climb up a tree out of danger and, as they rushed by, for my own safety I managed to hit one on the forehead with a big stone. It wasn't the best idea. It bellowed threateningly, lowered its head and ran straight through the fence, the other one following closely behind.

On they went, towards the school, and Robat went full speed on his motorbike to warn the teachers to keep the children inside until the animals were brought under control. Near the school was a convent and between the two buildings was a steep hillside covered with rhododendron bushes. Ieuan and I went in the Land Rover over to the convent, as we knew the bullock was headed that way. We were only chasing one by now.

How the creature managed to go over the school wall, I will never know, but I could hear a noise in the rhododendron bushes so I rushed to the convent garden, where a nun was sitting on a bench, reading.

'You can't sit there!' I shouted in panic. She raised her head, and looked at me as if I was a lump of dirt.

'Don't you know this is private property?' she said in a posh accent. 'You are trespassing. Get off this property at once.'

She was most unpleasant – I've never seen such an angry woman.

'Get off at once,' she repeated, whilst I was trying to explain what the problem was.

I could do nothing apart from repeating over and over 'You'd better move,' but she was ignoring me. The next minute a noise came from the rhododendrons next to the garden. She dropped her book in panic, and with one hand lifting her long dress and the other on her head, she ran as fast as she could towards the convent's door.

The bullock went through the garden without noticing either the nun or the convent. It ploughed on in a mad rush onto the road and towards the cemetery. It was then that I noticed a posh-looking woman walking her dog, which frightened me because I thought the dog might aggravate the bullock further, putting the woman in danger because it was completely wild. We were trying our best to corner the bullock and get it into the trailer.

By now Dad had gone ahead and had opened the gate to one of Trwyn yr Wylfa's fields, the property of my uncle Emrys Hughes, who was married to my aunt. Dad had seen him and had explained what was happening. We could do little apart from watching the bullock running wildly all over the road, past the woman and her dog thankfully, then – miraculously – through the gate and into the field.

We had virtually closed the school and frightened the living daylights out of a nun and a woman and her dog, but the bullock was still loose and wild. There was nothing for it but to phone the police telling them what was happening.

After a while, two experienced policemen arrived, two ex-army veterans, both carrying powerful guns. They explained that they wouldn't be happy for just one of them to shoot the animal in case they failed to kill it with the first shot. Both had to shoot, one aiming for the head, the other for the heart. They must have counted down before shooting, because I only heard one noise, even though they both fired their guns.

The bullock immediately fell to the ground, and didn't move an inch after that. It was stone dead.

Dad hates waste, and the animal was worth about £700. So we fetched the loader, raised it up and bled it before taking it to one of the sheds. Then we cut it up using a chain saw working on cooking oil so that it didn't taste of oil! After it had hung for three weeks, we paid a butcher to come and prepare the meat. We were all looking forward to enjoying a fat juicy steak because it was a fine beast. But no one managed to eat a single mouthful. The meat looked fine, but it wasn't right – it was what you'd call 'bone tight' – and had a nasty, sour taste. The dogs had a feast, though.

The bullock's temperature had soared whilst it was running wild, and three weeks of hanging made no difference whatsoever. The damage had been done when it was alive. It shows doesn't it, when you want to kill an animal for its meat, you have to do so quietly and calmly.

Yes, we lost that bullock because I had hit him on the head with a rock. But it was him or me, and it was better to lose the bullock – I think so anyway!

The wasps

Dad likes a bargain, and about ten years ago he'd bought a sheep and two lambs from Seimon, the village police sergeant who kept a few sheep in John the butcher's garden. One evening Dad wanted to fetch the sheep to bring them home.

I was exhausted after a long and hard day, and was enjoying five minutes at home with the wife. He came to hassle me, persuading, not ordering me, to go with him to the village. I protested that I was tired but in the end I had little choice, and there I was soon afterwards, knocking on the door of John the butcher and his wife, Bethan.

'Are the sheep and two lambs here?' I asked.

'Yes they are, in the garden somewhere,' said John. The garden was a pretty rough piece of land, with rhododendron bushes and brambles covering most of it, and I couldn't see the sheep anywhere.

At that time I had a dog named Craig – a very good dog, he could find a sheep anywhere. I sent him after the animals, but he returned without them.

'You'll have to go up there yourself,' said Dad, and I went grudgingly.

'I can't see them anywhere,' I shouted, squatting down in the thicket.

'Look up; they're in front of you!' Dad replied.

And I raised my head. Right into a wasp nest!

Well, you can imagine what followed. Llanfairfechan had never heard such swearing! I was wearing an old hood, and what I did – foolishly – was pull it tightly over my head trying to save myself. But the wasps were already inside the hood, and I made things much worse. I was covered in stings and scratches, and the wasps were everywhere, going down my neck and down my back, while I was thrashing about in the brambles. Next door to the butcher lived a respectable, chapel-going lady. I don't think she'd ever heard such language. I was swearing at Dad, at the dog, and at everything else in sight.

Bethan told me to put some vinegar on the stings, but I was so angry, I don't know what I told her when I heard that!

'I'm going home,' I said.

'Not without the sheep, you're not,' said Dad, with absolutely no sympathy! And there I was, until we collected the sheep. We bickered in the pick-up all the way home. I was swollen all over, feeling like the elephant man.

Rhian keeps bees, she has four hives, and I once heard Nain

saying, as a joke I thought, that rubbing onion on the sting was the best cure. But these were wasps, and their stings are worse. I learnt then that Bethan and Nain were both telling the truth. There's acid in vinegar and onions, and that acid helps neutralize the acid in bee and wasp stings.

But no amount of vinegar or onions could have stopped the torrent of swearing that night. It was all Dad's fault. The things you do for your family!

The Ghost

I am not a timid person and not easily scared, especially if what has frightened me can be explained. I recall, when I was young and attending the youth club, feeling a little anxious when walking along the dark road that led through the woods. My best friend at the time would usually come and meet me, and I felt better in his company.

I remember one night, when I was alone and walking past Ysgol Nant, hearing a baby crying. There was no one about and I had no idea where the noise was coming from.

A few days later I happened to mention this to Bob Bach Bwtsiar.

'It must have been a baby hedgehog crying,' he said. 'They make a noise exactly like a baby crying.'

Well I felt much better after that, having had a credible explanation.

But what do you do when something can't be normally explained?

I'm going back about 18 years now, when I still lived at home. There's a big building on the seafront in Llanfairfechan, a hostel belonging to the Christian Fellowship. The people who own it are rich, and it's rich people with their speedboats and Range Rovers who come to stay there.

One evening, just after I'd arrived home from my work on the farm, a young lad from the Christian Fellowship came to the door and asked if I had a big tractor. I told him I had, but that it was a strange question to ask. Then he said what his problem was. He and his friend were staying at the hostel and their speedboat had got stuck in the sand, and so had the Range Rover, and the tide was coming in towards them. There was no way they could move either the vehicle or the speedboat without the aid of a tractor.

I agreed to help them, thinking there was probably some money in it for me, and I asked what time they wanted me down at the beach. Half past two in the morning was the answer, after the tide had gone out. And he asked me how much the job would cost. I suggested £50. No problem, he said, and I immediately regretted not asking for more!

But it was still good money, and we went in search of ropes and chains, and Dad and I were down on the beach by half past two. The lad and his friend were waiting for us, and they told us the tide had gone out but that the boat and Range Rover were still stuck in the water and wet sand, so we waited for things to improve.

We had two strong lamps on the front of the tractor and they lit up an area the size of a football pitch as we went slowly towards the boat. We then reversed the tractor and the two back lamps lit up the beach. Suddenly, in the light, I saw a man crossing the sands. Not only that, I also had a strange and terrible feeling that I'd never had before, and I still shiver when I think of it. The man was wearing a vicar's collar, and I turned to Dad and said, 'That's a bloody ghost.'

'Don't be silly,' said Dad, 'he must be one of the Christians from the hostel.'

Yes, he'd seen him as well, but he didn't have the strange feeling that I'd experienced.

We proceeded to haul the boat up on to dry land, with one of the lads standing in the boat and the other walking beside it as we pulled it slowly away from the waves.

'Where's your mate?' I asked one of them after unhooking the boat.

'What do you mean?' he answered. 'What mate?'

'There were three of you on the beach,' I said.

'No,' he said, 'only two of us!'

'I told you, Dad, it was a ghost,' I said.

'Maybe you're right,' was the answer.

I know no more than that. I've never been superstitious, and I don't believe in ghosts. And yet, this strange feeling came over me when I saw the man crossing the beach. Even though it could have been someone from the hostel going for a walk, it was unlikely at that time of night, especially wearing a round collar. But I can't explain the feeling I got, a feeling I haven't had before or since and it was obvious also that the two lads from the centre hadn't seen anyone!

I never heard any stories about ghosts in the area, and I've asked around. Maybe someone will come to me with an explanation after reading this.

Yes, I've been frightened many times and I've usually been able to explain the reason. I got a big fright one night last winter. I'd drunk a lot of whisky with Dad and before we went to bed he asked me to go to check the cattle. There's a camera in one of the sheds, but not in the one where the cattle happened to be.

I never take a torch with me because I know the farm buildings like the back of my hand. I was about to enter the shed when something white shot out of the gloom and came towards me, missing my face by a couple of inches. I felt the wind on my face, and I was terrified. If it had hit me, I would probably have called it another ghost, but it was most likely a barn owl. We've had a barn owl here for years, since I was a small kid, and it breeds every year. Some farmers used to shoot them as they believed them to be symbols of bad luck and death, but I like having one on the farm and so do the children.

Yes, I believe there's probably a perfectly natural explanation for everything that frightens you, and that it is only imagination that converts natural phenomena into ghosts. But, there again,

I never could explain the white-collared man walking on Llanfairfechan beach at three in the morning, or the feeling of terror I had that night.

Pheasant shooting

If you work hard, it's important that you have a hobby, something that takes you out of your work environment for a few hours. That's how I regard pheasant shooting, something I've been doing for eight to ten years, and by now my sons accompany me.

A few of us started going shooting to Llwydfan farm in Conwy, my friends Wyn and Euros's farm, and by now there are 14 of us forming two teams of seven each. One team shoots and the other does the beating – this saves us from having to pay someone else to do it. Then it's all change for the next round. It's a good group; people like Gwyn Cynan, Steve Watts, Emlyn DPS and Emrys the Butcher. Every one of them is a very good shot, and one, Emrys, has represented Wales many times in shooting competitions. There are women amongst the shooters as well, and we do three stands in the morning and two in the afternoon.

One of the lads who used to shoot with us – but doesn't any more – is Embo Bwtsh, who has a very sharp tongue. I like to think that I'm pretty quick-witted, but I can't match him. I managed to match him once, however.

I'd had a good morning. I'm not the best with a gun, but I'd managed to shoot six pheasants. You shoot better on some days than others, depending on your mood, I suppose. This particular afternoon we were moving to another farm, Ty'n Coed, where there's an excellent stand. The shooter lays low and in front of you there's a big woodland and a lake, the habitat of wild ducks. This was the prime spot, where the pheasants fly up over the trees, and I remember that my cousin Robert, Gwyn Cynan, Steve Watts, Embo, Aled and Ali were with me on the stand. A few pheasants had flown over and one woodcock, and Embo and I had shot a pheasant each. His philosophy was 'If it flies, it dies.' He was a really good shot, never missed.

There's etiquette in shooting, as in any other sport. The rule is, if a pheasant flies in front of you, it's yours, but if it's between two, you must take turns to shoot. If the first misses, it's up to the second. But etiquette had gone out of the window that day. This pheasant flew up high in the air, and I think I missed it with my first shot. Then I heard another shot, Embo this time, before I emptied the second barrel and the bird fell to the ground.

All the shooters and beaters had seen the bird flying up over the trees. Embo was higher up the bank than me, and he was like a banshee, dancing and shouting with his gun in the air. 'That's mine, boys, that's mine! What a shot! When was the last time you saw something like that?'

But then I heard a small voice – my voice – saying: 'Hey, that was my shot.'

'Don't talk bullshit,' was his answer.

'Yes, I'm sure it was mine,' I repeated.

By now, everyone had gathered around, the children, the shooters and the beaters. And I thought that maybe I'd been stupid to open my mouth. It was only a pheasant, after all, one bird amongst many. But I was convinced I'd shot it!

'We'll pluck its feathers,' said someone. 'Then we can decide who shot it from where the pellets have hit. If they're on Embo's side, it's his; if on Gareth's side, the bird is Gareth's.'

That's what we did, we plucked my side first from the tail up – nothing. Then Embo's side – nothing. We moved on to the head, and just under the head, on my side, there were two pellets. It was my bird!

Well, he got some stick after that! But I don't think I could do the same again, I'll shut my mouth next time. I know it sounds childish, but if I hadn't said anything, he would have claimed the pheasant. I'm sure he was thinking that I was like a little dog barking at his heels. He doesn't shoot with us any more, he's with another shoot, but mark you, he's a hell of a shot! But good or not, that pheasant belonged to me.

Fight at the Split Willow

The occasion was Vicky's birthday, and it was shortly after Christmas. Vicky is my cousin Robert's partner, and Robert is Uncle Teg's son, and one of the company who works with me every day. The party was at the Split Willow, a restaurant in Llanfairfechan where many parties, weddings and other events are held. That was where Rhian and I had our wedding reception. Vicky's party was a hell of a good one, to begin with at least. Many members of the family were there – me, my brother Huw, Liam my second cousin, Robert's friends from Penmaenmawr, and also Vicky's college friends. They were rugby lads, but many of them were English, and some of them were real bastards to be honest.

They were a nasty lot; we took a dislike to them the moment we saw them. They sang 'Swing Low, Sweet Chariot' and we sang 'Stick your chariot up your arse'. All in all it soon became a bit tense, the situation being fuelled by alcohol, of course.

At one point Robat's friend Wayne was standing by the Christmas tree. He's a big lad, and so were all the rugby lads, about 15 of them, all around 20 years old.

One of them said something to Wayne, I don't remember what, but that was the spark that fired the whole place up. It was carnage – a real free for all with fists flying everywhere.

It wasn't long since I'd had a hernia operation and I didn't want any trouble. I was also wearing a nice colourful shirt, a Christmas present from Rhian, and I was very proud of it. No, I didn't want any trouble, but Huw didn't care about that. He's tall – well over six feet – and he can fight. If you're in a tight spot, he's the one to get you out!

Suddenly, someone grabbed me from behind, ripping my shirt. Well, that did it! About half a dozen of the rugby lads had gone to the back room and Huw, Liam and I went after them. The barman had lost all control of the situation and was hiding somewhere. Someone hit me on the top of my head with a bottle and I fell to the floor, with someone on top of me. I managed to get one leg free and I gave him a hard kick, and he also fell to the floor. He got up, but Huw smacked him in the face, grabbed him by his jumper and flung him out through the door.

By now, the others had had enough and they ran away towards the minibus. The barman was one of Huw's mates and he told us to scarper as the police were on the way. We were home by the time they arrived, and even though one or two were arrested, we escaped with no repercussions. Yes, that was a big night. It goes to show, you need to be careful who you invite to parties! Huw's my little brother, so I should be the one looking after him, but he took care of me that night. I was lucky to have him.

Me through my brother's eyes

Gareth and I are very different. We were quite similar when we were children – both of us having no interest in school work, but he went on to Glynllifon College while I went out into the world to make some money, working on the college farm and then on the A55. By now I have my own business but I still live in the midst of the farming community and I remain close to the family.

I was a bit wild when we were younger, and Gareth often got me out of trouble; he's calmer and thinks before he does something. He looked after me. He's very similar to Dad, a good talker. Dad can get up on his feet anywhere, a funeral, a wedding, anywhere, and speak. Gareth's like that as well.

He's happy in front of the camera which is a good thing as he does so much television work. He also understands farming, he knows how things work, how to get grants and about the latest developments in the farming world. Farmers will look anywhere for a grant – they'd accept a grant for going to the toilet if they could!

Gareth, like Dad, is a hard worker – he understands sheepdogs and is good at training them. We never fall out, we bicker, but we never fall out. He still treats me as his little brother, even though I'm much taller than him. I'm six foot four, but to him I'll always be Huw Bach.

As I said at the beginning, we all have to face various emergencies, but there's one that farmers fear above all else, one that deserves a whole chapter Yes, that's it – foot and mouth!

8

Foot and Mouth Disease

FOOT AND MOUTH disease is the biggest threat possible to any farmer because it attacks cattle and sheep. In 2001 it returned to Wales, 34 years after the last time it reared its head, in 1967, the year in which I was born.

For those with no link with the farming world and scant knowledge of it, and for many newspapers, the big story was the incredible sums of money farmers received as compensation for their animals. But this reflected the ignorance of the general public and the shortcomings of newspaper journalism. It was far from being the whole story.

There can be no worse experience for a farmer than to see his stock – a herd of cattle or a flock of sheep – destroyed, stock that has taken years to develop. No amount of compensation will get rid of the distress, the concern and the sadness of staring at empty field after empty field with no sound to break the silence.

The first alert that the disease had reached north Wales was a phone call warning us that foot and mouth had been found on animals at Gaerwen in Anglesey, near Plas Newydd, the Marquis's farm – the farm we had taken over less than a year earlier. On the farm were 600 of our sheep: ewes, rams and lambs. At the time Rhian was expecting our second child, and was nearing full term.

Dad, Uncle Teg and I used to go regularly to Plas Newydd to tend to the stock, and we received a phone call making arrangements for us to meet a vet there. He was an Australian and when he came he examined the sheep and he was unhappy with one of them. It showed signs of having contracted the disease, but this was no great surprise considering that the slaughterhouse in Gaerwen, where the disease was first discovered on Anglesey, was only a few miles away.

The vet said that he couldn't allow us to go home for fear of carrying the disease to the mainland. That came as a huge shock and I explained to him that Rhian was pregnant, within days of her due date. He promised to do his best, contacting his bosses to discuss the matter with them. We had plenty of disinfectant on the farm and we sprayed the vehicle and its wheels and ourselves, because the last thing we wanted to do was to carry the disease back home to Ty'n Llwyfan.

After some negotiation, we were given permission to go home, and when the vet re-examined the sheep he decided that it was healthy.

Two days later came the blow when we received a phone call saying the whole stock on Plas Newydd would have to be killed because the farm was within the culling area, the idea being to create a disease-free zone around the contaminated area in order to contain and confine it.

I'll never forget the killing. I know lambs are reared to be killed, but there's more than one kind of killing. These lambs were killed before their time, weeks after they were born, after we'd looked after them, making sure they were healthy. Lambing can be a very enjoyable time, looking after the animals, but seeing all those sheep being loaded onto the lorries on their way to the slaughterhouse in Gaerwen was a very upsetting experience.

We were not allowed to kill the sheep and the lambs ourselves, a vet had to do it, injecting each animal, and he wasn't very good at it. Indeed, Berwyn, the lorry driver threatened to report him unless he did a better job of it. We had to watch as newly-born lambs were killed, while the vet himself was totally heartless about it.

'Put ten in each bag,' he said. 'The army boys will be

picking them up and they'll be complaining if the bags are too heavy.'

I don't think that anyone can imagine the pain that everyone, not just us, went through during the time of the disease and the culling, and the compensation we got did nothing to ease that pain. No one received any money for the distress.

But the culling of the Plas Newydd sheep was far from being the end of the story.

The disease-free zone in Anglesey was cleared of all sheep and cattle, and Plas Newydd was of course empty. But those weren't the only sheep we had on the island. There were 250 wintering sheep and yearlings – the previous year's lambs – grazing at Ty'n Llan farm in Bodedern, and the owner, Rhys Hughes, was on the phone constantly because the time had come for the sheep to return home and he was anxious to turn his cattle out to graze.

But we weren't allowed to move the sheep to Plas Newydd or to our land in Llanfairfechan. We couldn't in fact move them anywhere, and yet the farmer had the right to use his own land for his own purposes. It was a catch-22 situation.

There was nothing for it but to phone the relevant office in Caernarfon to arrange a meeting and, as the company's secretary, I was the one who went there. It was the Friday before a bank holiday and not many people were working, but I got hold of an officer – I won't name him – and explained my problem to him. I told him that I had 250 sheep in Bodedern and was desperate to get them home.

The officer said that they'd have to be examined by a vet to ascertain that they were free of the disease before they were moved. Then he asked me where I wanted to take them. I showed him Ty'n Llwyfan and the other farms on the map.

'Sorry, but the land borders the mountain, you can't take them there,' he said.

So I enquired about Plas Newydd in Llanfairpwll. This was about three weeks after the cull there.

'Plas Newydd is now clear,' he said.

'Are you sure?' I asked.

He was certain of it, but to make doubly sure he went to get confirmation and he came back and said that everything was fine.

Because the bank holiday was upon us, we immediately went about getting a licence, filling the forms, obtaining the name of the vet who would examine the sheep – everything we needed to comply with the law. Then we phoned Rhys Hughes to tell him we'd be there on Monday to round up the sheep and take them away. I still have the licence that gave me permission! Glyn Edwards drove the lorry and we went to Bodedern, where Mr Jones, the vet from Anglesey, was waiting.

'Yes,' he said, 'the sheep are all perfectly healthy.'

So we loaded half of them onto the lorry and off we went.

It was a very strange feeling, driving through parts of Anglesey where there were no animals to be seen.

As we turned towards Llanfairpwll, Glyn asked me:

'Are you sure this licence is genuine?'

'Yes,' I answered. 'We've done everything they asked,' and on we went, turning off the road by the Pink Lodge and unloading the sheep on the farm. Then back for the other load, with the vet still there. Everyone was happy – Rhys Hughes was glad to get rid of them and we were relieved to have them back at Plas Newydd. And that was that – we were glad to have been able to save them in such difficult times for all farmers.

Or that's how we felt on Monday night! Tuesday morning came, and Dad received a call from the head of the department in Caernarfon.

'What have you done?' he said. 'You've tricked us – you've moved the sheep. You've already had your money and now you're wanting some more.'

Dad shouted at me: 'Bloody hell, what have we done?'

'Wait a second,' I said, 'I'll get the licence.' The licence had a number on it, and Dad recited the number over the phone.

'Error,' was the immediate response. 'The licence is incorrect.'

'That's a mistake your end,' Dad told him, 'and we won't allow you to kill these sheep, you understand.'

They were the best yearlings – year-old sheep – we had; they came from the Llyn yr Afon heft near Aber.

The matter was referred to the appropriate department in the Welsh Assembly, and we were told by officers there that they, rather than Caernarfon, would deal with the problem and sort it out. Dad was still stubborn, saying that on no account were the sheep to be slaughtered, and the television boys were on the phone constantly wanting to film an item while we wanted nothing of the kind – all we wanted was to keep the sheep alive. But a short report appeared in the *Daily Post*:

Error in Sheep Movement
224 healthy sheep are to be killed after they were accidentally moved into the Foot and Mouth disease slaughter area. The mistake was made by officials who gave permission for the sheep to be moved to a prohibited area. Carwyn Jones, the Rural Affairs Minister, has decreed that the animals must be killed.

That's how it was for a few days, phone calls from all directions, until one day we received a call from London. The matter had gone to the very top, and some high-ranking officer wanted to arrange a meeting with Dad and the rest of us in Plas Newydd.

As before, Dad, Uncle Teg and I went there and noticed, as we passed the lay-by before the Pink Lodge, that two or three livestock lorries were parked there.

Dad was still adamant that the sheep were not to be killed, while Uncle Teg was trying to persuade him that we were dealing with the law here, and that if the law said they had to be got rid of, we had little choice. But Dad was determined!

We arrived at the yard and saw a parked car, and out of it stepped a small, important-looking man in a light suit, a bit of a prat actually. And he asked us in English who owned the sheep, and Dad answered that they belonged to us, pointing at me, saying I was the shepherd. The man said that the sheep would have to be killed, and Dad told him that he couldn't do that. Things had started badly, a bitter argument was inevitable.

'It doesn't matter what you say,' the official said. 'You'll receive an official warning ordering you to kill them. You can do this the easy way or the hard way, it's up to you, but the sheep will be killed no matter what you do. Discuss amongst yourselves how much you want for them and come back to me to state your figure.'

Dad was still stubborn but Uncle Teg didn't want any more trouble. He saw that we had no choice but to give in to the system. He realised what would happen if the disease broke out in that area of Anglesey – we would be blamed for it.

'We'll demand a high price for the sheep,' said Dad, 'maybe he'll refuse.'

So we decided on a price that was well above their market value and we went back to the man to tell him how much we wanted, thinking he would at least reject our demand and try to bargain with us. Dad told him the price.

'Fine,' he said in his posh accent, with no hesitation, and he shook hands with Dad. But he warned us not to go to the press with the story, or reveal the price we got for the sheep.

Then he told us:

'Now you can go. These sheep are mine.'

As we were leaving Uncle Teg turned to Dad and said, 'We should have asked for more.'

That may be true, because thinking back, the price wasn't that high. But we were feeling deflated and knew, as we returned over the Menai Straits, that the killing had already begun, with the machines lifting the bodies and loading them onto the lorries as if they were nothing more than rubbish – a whole generation of sheep our fathers had worked hard for many years to rear. We knew it would take years to rebuild the flock – the best we had – the Llyn yr Afon flock on the Carneddau.

Believe you me, the compensation farmers had for losing

their animals during the foot and mouth period was not the whole story by a long chalk!

It was a phone call that broke the news of the disease to us, but thankfully there are more phone calls bringing good news than those bringing bad tidings, and it was such a call that led to a life-changing period for me.

9

Fferm Ffactor

I WAS WORKING with the sheep on Uncle Teg's farm, Plas Ucha, when I received the important phone call, a call from a Lowri Evans who worked for Cwmni Da, a Caernarfon-based television company. She said that the company was responsible for producing a series of programmes for S4C, *Fferm Factor*, and she asked if I was interested in taking part as two people had mentioned my name. I asked a few questions about the series and then thought, why not, I had nothing to lose. In for a penny, in for a pound!

So off I went to the showground at Llanelwedd on the first day of the Royal Welsh to meet officials from the company, and was interviewed before lunch in S4C's centre on the showground. I remember that it was before lunch as I had agreed to take part in a discussion on Dylan Jones's radio programme, *Taro'r Post*,[1] at twelve o'clock. At the interview I met two people, Neville and Non, and was invited to talk about myself for five minutes. I took ten! Well, what's new?!

A few days later I received an invitation to be one of the ten farmers taking part, and we all met up at the Marine Hotel in Aberystwyth to sign some contracts and obtain more details. It was a competition, a knockout, and I'm a competitive person, so it appealed to me. Most of the ten taking part were strangers to me, but I knew Geraint Siddall from Anglesey, had met Eleri

---

1   *Taro'r Post* is a daily Welsh radio programme where listeners have the opportunity to contribute to the discussions on matters of current interest.

before, and had come across Glenda at agricultural shows. From the start I felt that we were a close-knit group and indeed it stayed that way throughout the series.

Each one of us was asked about his or her criminal record and I decided that I had to come clean about my appearance at Merthyr Crown Court, but no one seemed to care about that. Afterwards we went home, to await the phone call that would tell us where and when the first venue would be. We were called to Glynllifon, near Caernarfon, for the first day of filming. The programme was presented by Daloni Metcalfe[2] and the judges were Dai Jones[3] and Wynne Jones.[4] It was a bad start for me in my relationship with Dai Jones. Me and my big mouth!

It was a Sunday, but I wasn't at my best. I had been to a wedding the previous day and it had been a late night. When we arrived we were ushered into a room at the top of the house. The ten taking part were three women: Morfudd, Glenda and Eleri; and seven men: Gareth (Roberts), Rhys, Aled, Geraint, Rhodri, Cefin and me.

It could have been my imagination but I had the impression that the film crew was eyeing us with suspicion, probably because we were rather cocky and strove all the time to try to find out what challenges the film company had in store for us during that day. But, throughout the filming of the series we weren't told until the last minute. Some of the tasks set were individual ones and others were team efforts. The individual tasks included getting a pig into a trailer, something that I hadn't done in 20 years; estimate animal prices, and answer some questions. My mind went blank on many of the questions, for instance the full title of 'CAP'. I could say

---

2   Daloni Metcalfe is a well-known presenter of a weekly farming programme, *Ffermio*, on S4C. She farms with her husband on the Llŷn Peninsula.
3   Dai Jones is a well-known Welsh singer and presenter of various programmes on radio and television. He farms at Llanilar near Aberystwyth.
4   Professor Wynne Jones is a former principal and chief executive of Harper Adams University College, Shropshire.

'Common Agricultural Policy' almost in my sleep, but it went from my mind completely during the first session of questions and I made a poor showing of it, which was most unexpected according to the judges.

The First Task

The first task however was to hang a gate, and we were to work in pairs, but weren't allowed to choose our own partners. I was with Aled Rees, who ended up winning the whole competition.

Off we went outside where wooden gates, poles and the essential tools for the job had been laid out for us. One pole had already been placed in the ground for each team, and our task was to hang the gate, position the receiving pole in the ground and close the gate. I believe we had half an hour to complete the task, and Dai Jones was the judge.

Aled and I worked well together, in fact all the pairs worked well together, but I considered that the women were at a disadvantage in this task because they weren't as strong as us, and digging a hole in the ground for the receiving pole was hard work as the ground was stony.

Whilst we were at it Dai walked around and observed each pair in turn. Time soon ran out and I felt that we had done a good job, everything had worked well and the gate hung level and closed perfectly.

Dai went to look at the first gate which Rhodri and Rhys had been working on. We could see all of the gates, and I thought that ours stood out in the way that it had been placed. Rhys and Rhodri's receiving pole had split when they tried to hammer the hook in. I would have thought that that was quite an error, but as Dai passed them he said that he was giving them the first prize. 'You have worked well together,' he said, 'and your gate closes well.'

When I heard this I felt my temper rising, but I didn't say

anything. Dai was judging and making remarks as he went from gate to gate and theirs was the first one he looked at.

He then moved on to Geraint and Eleri's gate. They hadn't done a brilliant job – the gate didn't close properly, so what Geraint did was put a piece of string around it and said: 'There we go, it closes just like the one at home now!' Yes, Geraint was a star!

Dai's attention turned to Glenda and Cefin next and he said that they had worked well together and gave them third spot.

He then came to us and Daloni asked him, 'What about this one?'

'Let's see,' he said. 'Does it rise well, is it level?' Then he said: 'Yes, it's perfect.'

He saw that it closed well too, and gave us second place.

Well, I'm a big mouth, and I probably should have learned to keep it shut. Daloni said to me, 'You don't look very happy.'

'No, I'm not. I think Dai needs new glasses!' I said cheerfully, but I meant it. I didn't believe that a gate that had a split pole deserved to win. And it developed into a debate, an argument even, and all this in front of the camera. They didn't show all of it on television, though!

Aled agreed 100 per cent with me that ours was the best gate. And after that I'm sure I didn't make a good impression on Dai because I don't think we were supposed to answer him back or disagree with him! But the way I've been taught is, if I feel something should be said, I say it. Even so, I'm still wrong quite often, and I've put my foot in it many times, but I believe that I'm right at the time and that I have the right to say what's on my mind, until otherwise corrected!

At the end of each programme everyone came together for the judgment, and to learn which unlucky one would have to leave the competition for good. Wynne Jones called five forward and announced that they were safe. I wasn't one of those five. Then Dai called another three forward and said that they were also safe. I wasn't one of those three either. Oh dear, things were looking bad. Then they called Glenda and me forward and said that one of us wasn't safe. My heart was in my throat. I could be the first to leave the programme, and I wanted to win! They then told us that no one was leaving the first programme. Everyone had a second chance – but only in the first programme!

'You have been very cruel,' I said, and wished that I was back home with my family.

I was safe for the time being, but if I was one of the bottom two on the basis of my performance so far, it was clear that I would have to improve greatly in the other tasks if I was to survive.

Rhug and Cerrig Show

We were given about a week's notice by the television company for the date and location of the next piece of filming. The second location was Lord Newborough's farm, Rhug, near Corwen. We had all survived the first round, everyone had been pardoned, and the ten of us had become good friends. There were a few good people within the television crew as well, especially Lowri who looked after us.

This time the first task was to cut half a lamb into cuts ready for selling; we were dressed appropriately, as health and safety regulations were strict. The butcher called in to judge us was Michael Thomas whom I knew well and had worked with him quite a lot, so he was shocked to see me. He obviously didn't know beforehand who the contestants were.

We worked in pairs, and my partner in this task was Rhys. To be honest, I had never cut a lamb; I had only seen my Uncle Wil and the butcher doing the cutting for us at home. But Rhys had been taught how and I think we did quite a good job after Michael Thomas showed us how it was done. We had some fun and joked around with some of the others, especially Rhodri Brynllech, he was jolly one, he had a big mouth like me. He was very funny and always had something to say. It's a shame that he had to leave when he did.

It was the women who were most successful in this task. I think they were concentrating more when Michael Thomas showed us how to do it. Aled also did well; he had been trained in butchering skills.

The next task, which was the first shown on the programme itself, and which was quite a fun task, was to drive a Massey tractor. I said that I had never driven one, but one of the lads got hold of my phone and it had a photo of me driving a Massey tractor on it! I was caught lying, and they kept taking the mickey after that. We had a good relationship and everyone enjoyed each other's company, having fun and developing friendship. It was early days and you wouldn't think that we were competing against each other.

I don't think that there has been the same close-knit relationship between the groups in the other series that have been shown – there was a special bond between the first series' group and we have been friends ever since. That's the impression that I got from watching the other series that have appeared on television, anyway. But maybe I am mistaken.

The tractor task went rather well. It was a challenge against the clock and we had to avoid various obstacles and only one or two failed in this task.

We were then driven to the bunkhouse – to Tomen y Castell, outside Bala, where we stayed overnight, and then taken by minibus to Plas yn Dre, Bala for a meal. The food there was fantastic, one of the best meals we had during the series. Rhodri knew the owner and we had a lot of fun there. The film crew had given us a camera and we were trying to lower the prices by pretending that we were filming for the programme, and so on.

We went on the town afterwards and ended up in Plas Coch hotel. I was disappointed to hear so little Welsh being spoken around the town, but maybe there were quite a few people on holiday there. We sang at Plas Coch and Eleri, Aled and Rhodri were excellent singers. Rhodri sang with Côr Godre'r Aran, the well-known male voice choir from Llanuwchllyn.

We had a fantastic night back in the bunkhouse, with two bottles of vodka and lemonade and a chance to sing! It was brilliant. It was between three and four in the morning when we went to bed – well, some of us. Aled went to bed before most of us and Geraint didn't drink. We had real bunks, one on top of the other, six or seven in one room. One of the lads jumped on top of Aled and he, under the weight, went through the bunk, with his bottom sticking out as the slats broke with a loud bang. But he took it well, thank goodness, although he was half asleep. We replaced what we could and hid the rest.

It was a daft idea to have such a late night with a competition the next morning, although we didn't know what it was. We were told that we were going to Cerrigydrudion's one-day agricultural show, and that the bus was leaving just after eight to take us there.

Cerrig has a good show and I remembered being there when I was younger. We got to walk around for a while with the camera crew filming us. We were all in our *Fferm Ffactor* jackets, and as it was a new series and everyone talking about it, people would come up to us for a chat. We felt like celebrities!

At the far end of the field there was a big *Fferm Ffactor* sign and a man from Bethesda whom I knew stood there. He was Dafydd Cadwaladr, a big strong man standing well over six feet, an axe man, but it was a saw that he had with him that day. I had worked with him many times in the past, and I asked him what he was doing there, and I remember that all our heads were banging after the vodka the night before.

Many people gathered around to see what was happening, and Dafydd showed us how to saw a thick tree trunk. He took 28 seconds to do it and I noticed that he was using every inch of the saw, pushing it forward to the end before pulling it back. That was one of the reasons why he was working so fast. I also noticed that it was when he was pulling the saw back that he was sawing, not when pushing it away from him.

This was the only task where we realised immediately who had won, as it was all a matter of timing. In most of the other tasks we didn't know who had won until afterwards, and that made us uneasy as nobody knew were they stood.

Cefin was a strong lad and he finished the task in 40 seconds. Rhys was strong as well, and so was Rhodri, and strength was a great help. Everyone was trying their best because everyone likes to win. Eleri gave up halfway through. To be honest, the women were again under a disadvantage, but Glenda carried on. There was quite a go in Glenda, and her husband Bryn and their little boy were there to support her, and the little boy was shouting to encourage his mother. It was my turn next, and a group of people whom I knew were watching, and I shouted, 'What would my wife say if she saw me now!' I beat Cefin by one second. Dai was the judge and he said, 'Gareth Jones is the best, the man who never stops talking, and he didn't stop sawing either.' Daloni kept the score and announced the winner. 'Hey,' I told Daloni, 'where's my kiss?' And she kissed me there and then, as a prize for wining, and the kiss was shown on the programme!

The disqualifying started for real at the end of the second programme. It was Rhodri and Eleri who were in danger, and Eleri was the one nominated by the judges to leave. It was a shame, but that was the game, and for the rest of us it was a case of moving on.

In Ewe-phoria

The third programme's tasks were held on the college farm at Aberystwyth, and there were no heavy physical tasks this time: labelling animal foods and estimating the weight and price of animals, cows and sheep. And then the task on the streets of Aberystwyth – selling cheese. Rhys was eliminated on this programme, leaving eight of us.

For the fourth programme, a few tasks with sheep were held

at Ewe-phoria Aled Owen's[5] farm near Llangwm. We stayed at the Owain Glyndŵr hotel in Corwen, a hotel run by a local Welshman, Ifor Siôn, a very pleasant man, and we received a warm welcome there.

The first task was to identify sheep breeds, and it was Aled and me who had the least success, we only got four or five marks. Aled got more stick than me as he had completed every other task so well. I didn't like this assignment at all, having to identify breeds like Torwen and Torddu which were mostly uncommon breeds, but Glenda and Gareth got them all correct.

Next came the shearing, which was fine for me. We all feel more comfortable in what we are used to, and I do my shearing in the old-fashioned way, not like these lads that go round shearing as they do, the Godfrey Bowen Style.[6]

The judge was a Scotsman, Doug Lamby, a hell of a nice lad, and he was accompanied by his wife, Ann. She did the talking as she's Welsh, born and bred at Ystrad, a farm in Llangwm, and she had returned home to farm with her husband after living in Scotland for a few years. Cefin had never sheared before, but he did a tidy job. Geraint, on the other hand, was an experienced shearer and felt that he was robbed in the final analysis. But he wasn't used to shearing in a competition and was judged for the double cut, which means not shearing close enough to the skin the first time, but rather tidying up by cutting the second time. The sheep looked perfect, but they took away some marks from him because of the double cut. Rhodri Brynllech won by a big margin; he was brilliant and well ahead of everyone else. He had done a lot of shearing,

---

5   Aled Owen is the foremost dog handler in Wales, having represented his country in internationals more than twenty times. He has won the Welsh Open Championship seven times and the World Championship twice, in 2002 and 2008. Among his other achievements was winning the doubles in the BBC1 series, *One Man and his Dog*.

6   This relatively new technique is less taxing on the back than the old-fashioned way.

having been out contracting. You have to take your hat off to someone like him who can complete a task like this much better than yourself.

We completed the last task with sheep at Ewe-phoria on the Sunday, before returning to Rhug to hear our fate. The last task was to separate them, and here I came head-to-head with Dai Jones again! We worked in two teams, setting up mobile pens – Prattley, a device from Australia – in the middle of the field and then herding sheep into it and separating the ones that had tags from the rest. In our team were myself, Aled, Rhodri and Morfudd, and I was elected by the others to be the captain, everyone saying that I had the biggest mouth! We were told that the team who completed this assignment in the shortest time would win. It was a task against the clock.

My work on the farm at home often comprises of sorting and separating sheep, herding them into pens and treating them, and I was familiar with Prattley pens. So we applied ourselves to the task in hand, Morfudd handling the dog, as she was used to sheepdogs, and because it was easier for us men to do the lifting and setting up.

Five minutes into the task I noticed that Morfudd was having difficulties with the dog. He wasn't responding to her at all and was all over the place, listening to neither voice nor whistle.

If a similar situation confronted me at home I would attach a rope to the dog and hold him back before he disturbed the sheep. But there was no rope available to tie him, so what I did was lift the dog up and put him under my arm, and we got the sheep into the pen and sorted them out in about 13 minutes.

We weren't allowed to observe the other team, and they weren't allowed to watch us. But Dai praised them, saying that they made the right choice by putting Gareth Roberts in charge of the dog, because a dog responds better to a man's voice than to a woman's. Dai actually said that my carrying the dog was a childish act. Well, all I can say is that I have trained dogs and dealt with dogs since I was a child, and every dog we have has been home trained. Dai buys dogs that have been trained by others, I train them myself! So I believe that I know more than him about them, and that I did the only thing possible in the circumstances as the dog was disturbing the sheep and sending them in all directions.

Gareth Roberts had some difficulties with his dog as well, but we didn't know that of course until we saw the programme. Their time was 14 minutes, so we were one minute ahead. As I said, we were informed at the outset that this was a task against the clock, but by the end of the competition and the programme itself, Dai, although he said that it was a timed task, declared that the other team had worked better as a team, and gave them first place. To my mind he had changed the rules along the way to suit himself.

Then back to Rhug for the judgment. They wanted a building with two big closing doors so that the judgment would be dramatic, and the one chosen to leave would look like he (or she) was walking out into the night, with the big doors closing behind him as he left *Fferm Ffactor* forever!

The feeling that I got while taking part in *Fferm Ffactor* was that it was a rollercoaster of a programme and that everyone was greatly missed by the other competitors when they had to leave.

Each one who had left was a real character. Eleri, who was the first to leave, was a great woman, small but intelligent, I've seen the stock on her farm. She's a mountain farmer, and the difference between us all was vast, ranging from milk farmers to mountain farmers. Eleri and I, for example, didn't do much work with tractors. But there is a disadvantage and an advantage to everything, and so it was in this competition. Eleri didn't have the chance to display her real talents; she was gone before we got to the sheep, which was her strength. She was very friendly and I liked chatting with her. You would have thought that she would be upset being the first to go home. I told her that I was very sorry, and her reply was: 'I've never been so glad.' She hated the cameras.

Rhys, the second to leave, was chatty and full of fun, a great lad. He was eliminated in Aberystwyth. He had milking cows, and he was young. He probably deserved to be eliminated because he didn't do very well in the Aberystwyth tasks. But again, he was greatly missed, and we felt his absence after he had gone. I know that's what the game was, and you felt glad every time that you were still in, nevertheless we missed everyone who had to leave.

It was Geraint who left this time, and he felt that he had been unlucky. I know that someone had to leave each time, but I also felt that he had been hard done-by. I had become very friendly with Geraint, he was the one that took his car everywhere. He came from Anglesey, so he would pick me up quite often, and as he didn't drink, he was usually the driver, and it was a shame that he left.

The Celtic Royal and Glynllifon

There were only seven of us left by the fifth programme and we were staying at the Celtic Royal (Celt) in Caernarfon, and filming at Glynllifon for the second time. Eleri, Rhys and Geraint had gone, and Morfudd was the next to leave. It was between her and Glenda, and in the part shown on the programme where the judges had a discussion, Dai favoured Morfudd and Wynne favoured Glenda. It was Morfudd who left, which makes you think that Wynne was the head judge or at least that it was his word that counted if there was a difference of opinion. Morfudd, as was the case with the rest of the women, was under some disadvantage, as some of the tasks required much physical strength, and we men had the advantage on those occasions.

We were filming for the whole of that Saturday, and on completion of one of the tasks an argument developed between me and the health and safety man. We were racing on motorbikes, racing around the track and doing various tasks for which we hadn't received any training or warning.

We were required to ride the bike to the bottom of the field, hook a trailer on, put the brake on, and turn off the engine before loading the trailer with bales and then return to the starting block by negotiating various obstacles, and ride over a pile of wood and then reverse the bike into a tight space. It was a task against the clock and time would be added on for each mistake, such as striking one of the obstacles, losing one of the bales on the way, and so on. The specialist for this task was the health and safety man and I think his name was Rhys Owen, and Wynne was judging. Wynne was a strong character, never saying much, but when he did say something you paid attention!

We were driven from the Celt to Glynllifon and put in a room to wait our turn. Nobody knew what the task was until it was their turn, and the ones that went before us weren't allowed to come back, lest someone spilt the beans, and we who were left got an unfair advantage.

I thought I had done a good job, had done everything right and that in good time. As I was driving towards the end there was a hump in the land, and I stood up and leaned forward. I'm used to riding a motorbike on all kinds of terrain, especially on the slopes of the Carneddau, and when I'm going uphill I always lean forward so that the balance is right. That's how I was taught and that's what I did in Glynllifon. It was second nature to me.

After I finished Daloni told me that I had forgotten to turn off the engine. Damn, that was true, and it cost me ten seconds. 'And you stood up on the bike,' Wynne said. And I answered that that's what I should have done, but the health and safety man didn't agree and said that I wasn't allowed to do such a thing.

'Yes, you are,' I said. 'Bloody hell, I have more experience than anyone here with motorbikes, and that on the slopes of the Carneddau, a hell of a dangerous place, and that's how I ride to be safe.'

'No, you're not supposed to do that,' he said, and it developed into an argument as I felt a bit annoyed about it. I think that Wynne regarded the whole episode as a bit of a joke, but Non, the producer, told me to leave it. 'Oh, I'm not finished with you,' I said to the man. But I had to return, of course, to the room with the others who had finished the task. That argument wasn't shown on the programme!

We had a bit of an argument amongst ourselves in the room afterwards, some of the competitors saying that they, the judges, must be right and would know the rules.

'I'm telling you,' I said. 'I can prove my point; I have a DVD at home showing you how to ride the new Honda in different places, on level fields and on slopes.'

I phoned Rhian and she said that she would bring the DVD to the Celtic Royal, and she did.

When we arrived back at the hotel, we saw Dafydd Iwan in the foyer, being interviewed by Radio Cymru. I had heard that Sain were having a party there, a party to celebrate 40 years since establishing the record company in 1969. I knew Dafydd as I had met him with Siân Wheldon when I was fighting the council election, so I took the opportunity to go and talk to him after he had finished the interview, and asked him what the party was and if there was any chance that we could join in.

He asked me how many of us there were, and I said seven.

'Yes, you can come,' he said. 'Come in later on.'

I said that we were going to the Black Boy for a meal and that we would be back later. It was in fact later than we had anticipated because we had such a good time there, chatting and bantering until it was nearly eleven o'clock and by the time we arrived back at the hotel, the Sain party was in full swing.

We went up to the door and told the security man that we had been invited. 'OK,' he said and in we went. And there was wine and food still on the tables.

Everyone was in high spirits, having had a bellyfull of

food and drink, and there was a good crowd of people there, including many famous names from the Welsh cultural scene. Then the singing started, with the MC for the night calling on people to perform. We all knew that Aled Rees had an excellent voice because when we went out as a group he would always sing. It was the singing that made social evenings so enjoyable for us.

I asked Dafydd if Aled could sing, and he agreed that he could, so I went up to the man with the microphone and told him about him. 'Who is he?' he asked. 'You'll soon find out,' I said. And Aled started singing and everyone was delighted. We all went up to sing afterwards and had lots of fun, and it was a hell of a good night lasting until the early hours.

But then came the next morning!

The DVD was in my hand when I went down to have breakfast. Aled and Cefin were at the table and on seeing the DVD Aled said: 'Don't be stupid, we've had a good night last night. Don't bother with them. Forget about it, it's past, it's not worth stirring it up.'

But I'm an obstinate so-and-so and I said, 'No, I'm going to take it to them, so that they can see for themselves.' And that's what I did. It was probably stupid of me but that's how I am. I believe, if you want to present your argument, win or lose, you must do so and be able to walk away with your head held high and feel that you've been honest and done your best. I don't know what they did with the DVD, but it obviously made no difference to the final judgment.

Dai Jones

While we were filming for the sixth programme at Llysfasi we were staying at The Castle Hotel in Ruthin and the judges, Dai and Wynne, and the TV crew were staying in the Castle itself – two different castles and two different standards of accommodation!

We received a phone call saying that there was a party at the

Castle, and as it was quiet where we were and nothing much to do around the town we decided to go – it wasn't too far to walk. When we arrived Dai and Wynne were drinking Drambuies in the hall.

We went to the bar but weren't allowed to buy drinks because it was only open to residents who bought their drinks on their accommodation card. I told Non the producer what the problem was and Dai, fair play to him, let me use his card to buy a drink. 'Buy everyone a round,' he said. And I did and still remember what the total was – it was £56!

We all sat together chatting away and there was a nice atmosphere there, everyone in high spirits and Dai was chatty too. And I thought to myself, if Dai had one more drink perhaps his tongue would loosen further and maybe he would start talking about the competitions to come and we'd get some information from him. So I had to think of a way of getting another drink as we weren't able to go to the bar and pay for it ourselves.

Cheeky of me, no doubt, but I suggested to Wynne that since Dai had bought us a drink, it would be nice for both judges to do the same. 'There you go, Jones,' he said and gave me his card, and I did the same as I did with Dai's card and bought everyone a drink. It wasn't as expensive this time, around £45 I think, including two double Drambuies for the judges!

We had been interviewed by both judges on that particular day. We had completed other tasks as well, welding and ploughing with horses, but the toughest task was the interview with both of them because two always have the advantage over one. We were asked why we wanted to be on *Fferm Ffactor*, how we thought we were doing and what we hoped to gain from the experience – matters like that, both of them asking tough questions, one after another.

I'm usually quite a good talker and I feel that I can stand my ground quite well. I guess I made quite an impression on Dai and Wynne because of that. Dai called me 'Mr Middle of the Road' and I complemented him on his contribution to agriculture. I was a bit of a creep, if you like, but everyone likes to be praised! Both judges asked me what my weaknesses were and I said that I'm a stubborn individual, determined. I also said that I came into the competition as myself, and I would leave as myself as well.

'You will love it if you reach the final,' Dai said to me in the Castle.

'Why do you say that?' I asked.

'Well, you like to talk and argue, and the last task will be to talk to someone important in the Assembly Government.'

He said no more, but he didn't need to. I was almost certain that I knew who the important person was going to be. It could be none other than the then Minister of Agriculture, Elin Jones. And as it transpired I was right – it was her! But I had to reach the final first!

Yes, we had a good time that night, one of the best. But there was a shock awaiting us at the end of the sixth programme. It was between Glenda and Rhodri in the judgment and the other four of us, me and the other Gareth, Cefin and Aled were safe for the time being. The shock was that two had to leave, probably because no one had left at the end of the first programme. I have to say that the two were greatly missed. The longer you stayed in the competition, the closer you got as friends, although it was a competition. Rhodri was a star, a very jolly lad, and Glenda very determined, holding her ground against everyone and doing her best in every task.

It was a shame that they were gone – but I was still in! For the time being at least, and the hope of winning was still alive.

Kick Out

So there were four of us left, by the time of the next location, down south somewhere, south of Aberystwyth and that is why the other Gareth (Roberts) and I were staying at a hotel because the two others lived in the vicinity. After Gareth had gone to bed because he was tired, I was standing at the bar talking to some of the local lads when *Fferm Ffactor* was shown on the TV. One of the lads recognized me from the programme told and me that we were going to a farm up the road the following day to an auction, a geese and bric-a-brac auction, and I thought he was pulling my leg.

The others arrived in the morning and we sat drinking coffee for over an hour and half – there was a problem and we were told that the task, whatever it was going to be, wasn't going to work and that they had to find another task for us.

So, not long afterwards we went in our cars towards Aberystwyth without knowing exactly where we were going. But we weren't far from Llanilar where Dai lives, I remembered the road.

We ended up in a field where there was a massive tractor with a hedge cutting machine attached to it. We knew then that the task was to cut hedges and thorn and we were shown how to do the job. The driver was introduced to us as John, and we then realised that he was Dai Jones's son. I regarded that as quite odd – one of the judges' sons taking on an important role like this. But having said that, there had been a problem and something had to be done. And it must be said that John was fine and there was no problem with him at all.

We had a quarter of an hour to do the job but I'm sure that Cefin, the first to go, finished in eight or nine minutes and John gave him seven marks. I was next, and I was given a score of three and was judged harshly – I was slated to tell the truth. Well, I had never cut a hedge with a tractor before and I made quite a mess of it to begin with, I went too far into the hedge, and then left some thorn there, but I thought I had done quite a good job overall and I had three or four minutes of my time left. But when Daloni told John that this was the first time I had cut a hedge with a tractor, he added, 'And the last time, I hope!'

Gareth was next, and he was in and out of the hedge quite a lot. I didn't think that he was much better than me and he ran out of time, but he got six! Aled was the best by far, he was excellent, he was an old hand at going out contracting. His work was worth seeing and the judge gave him nine marks.

I must say, if I was an official judge in a competition, I would never choose my son to judge a part of it. It's true that they had a problem, but it was Dai's idea, and the media accepted the idea without thinking twice in order to get them out of an awkward situation.

After we had done, off we went to Dai Jones's farm, and I must admit that we had a very warm welcome from Dai and his wife Olwen, and were immediately made to feel at home there.

But there was another task awaiting us, which was to judge Dai's Welsh Blacks. He had put three of his cows in a specific order and we had to try to place them in the same order. To be honest, I was quite disappointed with the standard of the three cows. I did quite a good job and chose the correct one for the first position, but put the other two in a different order, and Gareth and Aled did the same. It was only Cefin who put the three in the same order as Dai.

By now I had a strong feeling that my time on *Fferm Ffactor* was coming to an end, and it didn't come as a shock to me when I was eliminated. It was between me and Gareth and it was me in the end, with Cefin and Aled still safe.

I would have liked to have had the opportunity to talk to Elin Jones and present my ideas to her, but it was not to be. I didn't think I was going to win, but it would have been nice to reach the final. Going out was a strange feeling, it was sad and disappointing, but also there was a feeling of relief that it was all over. And I'm glad that I didn't sell myself short by taking part, and had been myself all along. The competitors were a fantastic group of people and I made some good friends and I left the competition not having demeaned my character.

Being a part of the series didn't do me any harm at all. I had previously been on Griff Rhys Jones's programmes *Mountain* and *Big Country*, and nothing had come of those. But this programme was different, and in the wake of it came *Snowdonia 1890* and then *Countryfile* and the *BBC Young Farmer of the Year* and *Wales in Four Seasons*, and all of it growing like a snowball. I have to say that I have never gone after anyone to be on these programmes, they have come after me, and I owe a big thanks to *Fferm Ffactor*.

10

Snowdonia 1890

PHONE CALLS AND personal contacts – two things that can radically change lives. Certainly in my case, they were the two factors that resulted in my participation in the television series, *Snowdonia 1890*.

Those of you who viewed the programmes on BBC1 will remember that it was a series that followed the trials and tribulations of two families chosen to live in the severe and unwelcoming uplands of north Wales in 1890 conditions.

The phone call came from a girl called Lowri Jones, and the personal contact was the fact that she was a college friend of another Lowri – Lowri Evans, *Fferm Ffactor*'s researcher. The one Lowri phoned the other one to say that she was looking for a farmer or shepherd to take part in *Snowdonia 1890* and asking if she could suggest a name. Lowri said she could – me, and gave her my phone number.

I was given the bare bones of the series over the phone and invited to Galeri, Caernarfon, for an interview. Several characters were required for the series – a minister, schoolmaster, gamekeeper, Sunday school teacher, butcher, shopkeeper, several quarrymen and a farmer who was also a shepherd!

Three people interviewed me, two women, Siân Price and Vicky Rogers, and one man. I remember the women's names but not the man's – though he did most of the talking. The whole interview was in English and was recorded on film.

They asked me about my farm and my work and what I

thought of the proposed series. They said they would need me for five days of filming and gave me the dates. The dates suited me – five days in the period before the lambing season, and I felt that the interview had gone well. The money was quite good for five days' work, and that was a bonus.

As a last question the man asked me what would be my greatest disadvantage if they offered me the part of a 1890s farmer. He wasn't smiling but I ventured a wisecrack – 'I think I'm too good-looking for the job!' The two women nearly fell off their chairs but there wasn't the flicker of a smile on the man's face, and I was kicking myself for shooting my mouth off after such a good interview, telling myself that my bloody cheek would lose me the job.

They said that they'd be in touch before the end of the week and I went off home convinced that I'd lost the part. Rhian asked me how it had gone and I told her exactly what had happened. She was mad at me, but knew that's how I am and that I'm not likely to change!

A week later Lowri phoned to offer me the part, and I accepted. They needed my measurements to kit me out in the appropriate clothes, before I went to meet the producer, Ceri Rowlands, on the film set in the mountainous terrain above Rhosgadfan. The first day was spent getting the clothes right for the period. Every garment had to be authentic – the vest, shirt, jacket, coat, leather belt, leggings, and cap. When everything was on I felt as if I'd been kitted out for the North Pole!

We were then taken up to the two cottages, one of them had stood there since the 19th century, the period depicted in the series, the other one was built of wood and scaffolding, especially for the programmes. They looked exactly the same, it was quite uncanny.

I was told that two shorthorn cows were coming across from Chester that very day, Saturday, and that I'd have to hang around until they arrived to make sure that conditions were right for them, and to milk them, as the two families would not be arriving until the Monday.

The farmer who brought them wasn't very happy with the shed or where his cows were to be tethered. I told him that I would look after them as if they were my own cattle, and I have always believed that when one gives his word it must be kept.

A great friend of mine, Rhys Owen, head of agriculture and conservation at the Snowdonia National Park, had come to give me a hand and we milked the cows before going home. Our headquarters was situated in a building belonging to Mountain Rangers, the local football club. The film crew had a huge articulated lorry there to store all the costumes and the cooking equipment, because in all there were over 30 people involved and they were there for three whole weeks. It was like a mini village.

The following morning, Sunday, Rhys and I went up again to milk the cows and the BBC production team had already arrived. A company called Indus was to film the series, but BBC Productions were responsible for all the advertising work. Both companies needed me at the same time. While the BBC were taking pictures of me for the advertising schedule – and they were really good pictures – Indus called to say they needed me, and I was pig in the middle having a whale of a time. I'd never before had two women fighting over me!

All Indus wanted me to do was to stand, ominous-looking in silhouette on the top of the mountain in my shepherd's rigout watching the families come up by horse and cart. There were two cameras filming the scene, and I stood there for over an hour until my lips were blue with cold.

Then I had to go down to be introduced to the families as I was their next door neighbour, as it were, who would help the wives if they had trouble with the sheep or cattle whilst their husbands worked in the quarry.

All this was filmed and I had no script – they wanted everything to be as natural as possible.

So off I went to meet the first family, the Braddocks. There were cameras and equipment all over the place and they expected me to ignore the whole paraphernalia. It wasn't easy, I can tell you.

The family were standing in the doorway of their cottage and I went up to them.

'Sut dach chi?' I asked, taking it for granted that all the families in this part of the country at the end of the 19th century would be Welsh speakers. But they were not, so I had to greet them in English.

The Braddocks, Mark and Alisa and their four children – Jamie who was 19, Jordan, 16; Tommy, 13; and the youngest, Leah, 9 – were from Abergavenny. The other family, the Joneses from Denbigh, were Welsh speakers – David was a solicitor, Catrin his wife a tribunal officer, and they had three children, Ben who was 18, Ela, 11; and Jac, 9.

I didn't have much time to get to know them before having to familiarise them with the cows and the milking process. My immediate reaction to Alisa Braddock, a fine-looking lady, was that she was the flirtatious type who liked men and knew how to get her own way with them. She was a drama school teacher and loved acting. Her husband was a mechanic in the ambulance service and neither of them or their children knew anything about farming. The family were a mix of relationships: Jamie was Mark's son but not Alisa's, and Jordan was Alisa's son but not Mark's, and he did not live with the rest of the family.

I soon learnt that Jamie had very little interest in what was going on. They had been brought together just to make the programme, and there were tensions between some of the family members – which was of course great for television.

None of them had any idea how to milk a cow. The women would be doing the milking and Catrin Jones tried her best and was eager to learn, as indeed was her husband, David. Ela tried to help her mother and she moved the bucket which was half full of milk to within reach of the cow's foot. The cow of course kicked the bucket and the milk was spilt all over the place. Catrin snapped at her and Ela bawled her eyes out. What a good start to the series, I thought, and of course the cameras were recording everything.

But it must be said that both families managed to finish the milking eventually, and I went off home feeling quite confident that the day had gone fairly well.

Monday morning dawned and I was back at the cottages to supervise the milking and found that they had managed quite well. Then back to the site to change and call at the office. The producer, Ceri Rowlands, asked me how the families were doing and I praised the way they were coping. But she told me that I was helping too much and that I should let them struggle and make their own mistakes.

I wasn't sure how to take this, but on reflection I saw her point. The series was meant to show two families coming to terms with 19th century way of life and I was only there to help and support them, not to do the chores for them.

So I went home, but at half past six that evening they phoned me to go up there immediately as a problem had arisen. I was dead tired, what with going back and forth to the cottages and working at home on the farm, and it was 40 miles from Llanfairfechan up the mountains to Rhosgadfan. But up I went, changed into the usual rigout and went up with one of the runners to see what was wrong.

And what a mess! No one had cleaned the shed, a daily necessity, and there was cow muck everywhere. I had impressed upon them the importance of cleanliness, to keep the cattle healthy and free from mastitis. The two cows had been in all day, and as cows do, they'd made a terrible mess. The two families had ignored my instructions.

I shouted at Catrin and she didn't take it too well, and to add insult to injury, the cow stood on her foot. But, to be fair to her, she did go to the Braddocks to tell them that I'd given her a right bollocking for failing to keep the cattle clean.

Mei, the cameraman, knew that I was angry and he saw his chance. He asked me to record an interview, which was included in the programme, emphasising the fact that they had to pull together and do things properly if they wanted to stay the course. And that's how the first programme ended, with me telling them to work as a team if they wanted to survive a month on the mountains in such conditions. I wasn't doing it just for the television – I was bloody mad with them for dragging me back and forth like a yo-yo.

I wasn't called out on Tuesday, so I was able to catch up with some work on the farm. Come the evening – another phone call – the Braddocks hadn't milked. I was by now beginning to think that I'd been talking to myself up there. I was livid. I jumped into the car and went straight to the office and told them that I'd given my word to the owner that I would make sure that nothing happened to his cows.

Anyway, I changed and went up to find the Jones family busy milking and everything looking shipshape. It was a different story with the Braddocks's cow. She hadn't been milked, she had no hay, and she had fouled her water supply. When I got to the house they were all sat at the table eating their supper!

I was angry and I pitched into them, saying that this was no way to live on the mountain. Alisa got up and ran out crying. I followed her and told her that her tears were wasted on me and that she should get the children to help by fetching clean water and some hay. I told them that the milking had to be done before supper, that looking after the cow had to be their priority, and that they had the whole evening afterwards to stuff themselves to their hearts' content.

Then the husband started to make threatening noises, and I thought for a moment that he was going to physically attack me. I'd obviously underestimated him. But I was really angry. Eventually everyone cooled down and the cow was milked. This family seemed to have no interest in the project, blaming the poor cow for everything – as if she could help it!

Her teats were tender because they hadn't understood how important it was to milk her at the same time every day, and that a supply of clean water was essential for her. They were a family full of tensions, whereas the Joneses were a strong family unit, used to pulling together.

The next day, Wednesday, the sheep had to be brought in to be marked and that turned out to be a shambles. They each had six sheep and I, with my dog, could have done the job in a few minutes, but of course the film crew wanted them to do it themselves. The poor sheep were chased all over the place, and I kept telling them that they were heavy with lambs They belonged to Glenda from *Fferm Ffactor* and I'd promised her that I'd keep an eye on them.

The family members had no system at all, the children were all in the wrong places and Jamie just sullenly stood there, doing nothing. Eventually they managed to get them all into the shed, but not before the television people got what they were looking for, the sheep running wild all over the place, jumping hedges and fences and chased by both families.

The children enjoyed tending the sheep, checking their feet and mouths, and I went home thinking that the day was over. I was wrong, the phone rang. The Braddocks hadn't milked their cow again!

Another quick turnabout and I was back at the cottages again. The cow looked fine, she had clean water and hay, but of course she hadn't been milked! It was a wet dreary day and when I went into the cottage they said that they were on their way to do the milking. I told them to get on with it immediately, and that I wouldn't be coming up again if they were in trouble. If anything else happened they would have to shoulder the blame, and would have to face the consequences themselves.

At long last they were beginning to take notice, probably because of my threat not to turn up again to help them. Anyway, I had no more trouble with them for the rest of their stay – except for one of them on the football field.

One day Lowri phoned to say that she was staging a football match to be included in one of the programmes in the series, and asking me if I would play. I wasn't too keen, I hadn't played for years, but when she said that Alun the quarryman and the series' gamekeeper were playing, I said that I would give it a go. However, the gamekeeper never showed up – damned lucky for him!

Alun and I and the two families were to play against the local team – Mountain Rangers. We were kitted out with the appropriate clothes for the period, including shorts that reached well below the knees. We did look a sight! Our team were one short because of the gamekeeper not turning up, so Mountain Rangers, a team of Welsh speakers, and big strong lads to boot, allowed us to include one of theirs, Benji, quite a star, in our team. The referee, a nice, pleasant man, had no idea what lay ahead of him.

The families arrived with the children looking forward to the game, eager to do something different to their usual routine in the series. They said that Jamie had played a lot of football, that he was indeed a semi-professional, and Ben was a rugby player. But they were all keen to have a go and ready for a bit of fun.

When the game started Mark Braddock, the father, went at it hammer and tongs, dashing about wildly, tackling dangerously as if he was trying to work something out of his system. But the local lads didn't let him have his own way – they soon had the measure of him and a fight ensued, a real humdinger with Jamie trying to stop it. Mark was sent off the field, but when he came back he was even worse, persisting in targeting one of the Rangers team. A supposedly friendly affair became a match full of tension! And some of it was shown on the programme.

Mark completely spoiled what was supposed to be a bit of fun. Jamie got a kick on the knee and could barely walk. I was kicked just below my backside and my leg was black and blue from top to bottom by the following day. It was a shambles and the Braddocks were thoroughly ashamed of Mark. I think that it was so much tension in the family that made him kick out and behave like a wild animal on the field.

On the last Saturday, with only a day's filming left, we all went to chapel. The service was recorded on the Saturday, but it was Sunday in the programme. Marcus Robinson was the preacher and he is quite a character. He acted as minister in the service, and he is actually the minister in Llanrug. I was in my Sunday best, complete with top hat, and after the service the families went back to their cottages and I went down to the site to change.

Soon I saw a helicopter circling above the mountains, but thought nothing of it as it is quite a normal occurrence up in the hills. But just as I was getting out of my suit, Eleri, one of the runners, came down in her car at top speed. When she saw me she shouted:

'Come, come at once.'

'What's up?' I replied.

'Ben has been injured by the cow.'

'Badly?'

'We don't know. He's flat on his back in the shed.'

Up we went. When I reached the shed, the cows had been taken out, the film crew had called the air ambulance and it was still circling above, and the boy was lying on his back in cow muck. He looked pale and was perfectly still and everyone was afraid to move him in case his back was injured.

The families had been milking the cows outside and then leading them into the shed to tether them up. Mark Braddock had milked the cow, taken her in, but hadn't tethered her properly. Ben was in the shed and when the cow became free and tried to get out, she crushed Ben against the door post as she went.

The helicopter was about to land, so the cows had to be caught. I was still in my chapel suit and fancy boots and the cows were very agitated, but the job had to be done.

Catrin was very upset when the paramedics came and started to treat Ben – well we were all upset, not knowing how badly he was hurt. She said she couldn't think of milking and, because there was only a day's filming left, I suggested that there was really nothing to lose if the cows were returned prematurely to their owner. The two families had managed to stick it out for the whole period although they were all townsfolk, and they'd had quite a hard time of it.

Ben was taken to Ysbyty Gwynedd and kept in overnight. There were no broken bones, but he was badly bruised and in a lot of pain. But he returned the following day to finish the series.

Months later, sometime in the autumn Rhian and I were invited to a reception at Seiont Manor Hotel, Llanrug, where there was plenty of food and drink and what they call a screening, showing short episodes of the programmes. The first thing I saw when I walked in was a huge poster with me in shepherd's clobber on it. It was a damn good picture and I hadn't seen it before.

I then took part in many interviews, and as a consequence my picture appeared with a feature in the *Daily Post* and *Western Mail* when they publicised the series before it was shown.

Following the interviews we were shown some scenes from the programmes. There were several bigwigs at the reception, including Hywel Williams, the local MP, and several important people from the BBC.

When we went to the bar a lady who was talking to one of the owners of Indus, Paul Islwyn Thomas, came up to me and said that she'd seen rather a lot of me recently. She turned out to be the editor who had gone through every frame of film that was recorded to choose what to show in the series.

Paul asked me if I had any suggestions about the project and I said that if they considered making another series they should get the families in beforehand, say for two days, in order to teach them to milk and look after the animals.

The editor turned to Paul and said:

'But that wouldn't be good TV would it?'

And I said:

'Now I know how ruthless you are,' because I was thinking of the animals' welfare.

But it was true. They only wanted good programmes, and they wouldn't be good if everything went smoothly and there were no problems at all.

One good thing to come out of the series was getting to know new people and making new friends, like Derek (who sadly is no longer with us) and Ann, the two who were responsible for the Mountain Rangers football team. I also made friends with the back-up family who were there in case one of the families pulled out before the end of the filming. They were Jonathan and Lisa Fearne from Carmarthen, and we later stayed with them when the Urdd National Eisteddfod was in that town.

I enjoyed myself – I was under no pressure and the film crew were a jolly lot, many of them Welsh speakers. I hope I came over fairly well, although many people told me afterwards that I was 'a nasty old bugger'. But I think it showed farmers in a good light, showed the viewers what we have to put up with, and what we do from day-to-day. We still do so many things that farmers did at the end of the 19th century, except that we have electricity and better living and working conditions nowadays.

11

Llanfairfechan
and its People

I HAVE ALWAYS lived in Llanfairfechan, and this is where I will remain. I've been a councillor for the last four years, and was mayor in 2012, and publicising the town and attracting visitors is an important aspect of the work, as well as tackling problems and bringing pressure to bear on higher authorities to act. I initially went on the council when I realised that if we Welsh people don't take the initiative, the place will soon be run by incomers. We the Welsh are rather good at moaning about everything, standing on the sidelines, and not doing anything about it ourselves.

Llanfairfechan is a very interesting place to live in, and this chapter is about the people who live here and some of the local activities.

Siân Wheldon

Siân is one of the people who helped me a lot when I was campaigning the first time for a seat on the council – she had just bought a house in the town at the time. I was contesting the election for Plaid Cymru and had received some help with my pamphlet but, in the main, I wrote it myself and it was printed locally.

The next step was to distribute it around the town. It had a section for people to note down any problems they had, and then return it to me so that I could get to know what was worrying them. Several were returned complaining about holes in the road, unemptied bins, that sort of thing. One came from Siân Wheldon, complaining that water didn't drain away in front of her house, and at the same time drawing attention, in a kind way, to several mistakes in the Welsh section of my pamphlet!

Although I didn't know her personally, I decided that she was worth a visit and one evening I knocked on her door. She was very welcoming and promised to help me write my stuff and take the leaflets around town. She also said that she and Phil Edwards, the leader of Plaid Cymru on the county council, would accompany me around the town on election day. She also came with me to the count in Conwy, and she knew everyone there, all the councillors and, it seemed, everybody else! Of course they all knew her as Sandra Picton from *C'mon Midffîld*.[1]

Siân opened so many doors for me, and it's quite true that when you get to know someone, you get to know so many more. That's how I met Dafydd Iwan, and through him, as you already know, we were allowed into Sain's celebration party in the Celt when filming *Fferm Ffactor*.

I enjoy being a councillor, it gives me an opportunity to serve my community, and give back some of what I've been given all my life.

Islwyn Parri and William Hughes

Islwyn Parri was the headteacher of Ysgol Tryfan, Bangor, when I was a pupil there. He was an excellent head, and a very pleasant person – I'm sure he deserved much better pupils than

---

1   *C'mon Midffîld* was one of the best and most popular comedy TV series in Welsh. It is still shown, and is as durable as *Fawlty Towers* in English. Adapted from a radio series, the television programmes traced the story of a local football team, and the many hilarious experiences of team members. The barmaid in the local pub was Sandra Picton, daughter of the pompous team manager, and the part was played by Siân Wheldon who was then a full-time actress.

scallywags like me! His father-in-law, William Hughes, a lovely man, lived with his wife Annie at Rose Mount, Llanfairfechan, and he was the best sheepdog trainer ever. He and my father were bosom pals and he taught me a great deal about sheepdog training, and about life in general. Being retired, he had more time than Dad to come out to the fields with me. William Hughes was a quiet, gentle man, never angry or irritable, and a great friend to my family throughout his life.

When we were kids, Huw and I were always glad to see William Hughes coming to Ty'n Llwyfan because he always brought us sweets. He trained my first dog, Sbot. Poor old Sbot! Dad gave him to me when I was about twelve and I won many trophies with him in under-21 competitions at sheepdog trials and shows. But one day he hanged himself on his chain trying to jump over a gate. After that we had proper kennels made for the farmyard dogs.

I was probably disciplined less often by Islwyn Parri than I deserved in Ysgol Tryfan because of my association with his father-in-law, as I was constantly getting myself in top trouble. The truth is that I wasn't too keen on school, I just wanted to be home on the farm, and Dad didn't put much pressure on me either. By now I regret not making the most of my schooling, and I try to instil its importance in my own children, because things have changed, and farming has changed so much. There was hardly any paperwork involved when I started farming, how different things are today!

My primary school was Pant y Rhedyn School in Llanfairfechan, and I remember my teacher there, Valmai Griffiths, a marvellous teacher, but we were all afraid of her. Then I went to Ysgol Tryfan, Bangor, and the school grew with us. We were the first pupils there, and many of the children had a farming background. The Welsh speakers all tended to go there, but there were also kids from English-speaking families, from places such as the Maesgeirchen area of Bangor. It was a happy school, not too big to begin with, and we were a very happy crowd. Very few of the pupils who were there with me from Llanfairfechan still live in the area – they are spread all over the globe now. My children also have their schooling in Bangor, they go to Ysgol y Garnedd and Ysgol Tryfan, both Welsh-medium schools. The Llanfairfechan local school became very anglicised when the town, previously in Gwynedd, became part of Conwy, but I think things may be getting better there these days.

Training Dogs

There is a 26-acre field called Cae Llwyn Sgolog in Llanfairfechan, and this is where the annual sheepdog trials are held, and where I train young dogs in the evenings when I've finished on the farm for the day.

One summer's evening a few years ago I was training a very promising dog, one who responded to every command – whether it be sending him to the left, or the right, or stopping him in his tracks. I had sent him to round up the sheep, and then commanded him to stop. He obeyed immediately, but then I heard another whistle from somewhere, and off he went like a shot. I thought nothing of it and carried on, sending him left and commanding him to skirt the field, and once again he obeyed. Then there was another whistle and he stopped again. This happened over and over, every time I whistled a command, another one came from somewhere and the poor dog didn't know whether he was coming or going, and I had to call it a day before I got mad with myself and with the dog.

I thought it might be an echo, but I had never heard an echo before in all the years the sheepdog trials had been held there, and during all the years since we had bought the field and had been training dogs there.

Some time afterwards there was a 50th birthday party for Cedric Thomas at my Uncle Emrys's farm, Llys y Gwynt. His daughter Nia is Cedric's wife and he's a well-known trickster. You know what's coming.

I was talking to him at the party and he said: 'I don't see you training your dogs on Cae Sgolog as often as you used to.'

'I'm there whenever I have a free evening,' I answered.

'I noticed you there some time ago and you only stayed about five minutes. What happened?'

'Why do you ask?'

'Just wondering what went wrong.'

'There was an echo there.'

And I knew what he was going to say.

'It was me, hiding behind the wall and whistling. I expected to see you lose your rag with the dog.'

'Sorry to disappoint you, you old devil,' I said.

That's when I realised that when someone tricks you and you don't mention it to anyone, the truth will come out in the end, and it's usually the perpetrator himself who spills the beans. If he'd been cleverer he could have held his tongue and repeated what he'd done for a week or two – that really would have had me puzzled.

Dr John's Party

When I was in my late teens I used to go to a lot of parties, including many at Bryn y Neuadd, the nursing home for people with mental disorders which was just down the road, and where many nurses from all over the world came to be trained.

Dr John worked there. He wasn't really a doctor but was called that because he sounded like one. He was actually a staff nurse and he lived in one of the Graiglwyd flats down in the town. He loved parties and that was great for us young lads.

One day he invited me to one of his parties, not in Bryn y Neuadd itself but at his flat, and he told me to bring a couple of cans. My cousin Ieuan and I had been seeing two quite pretty young nurses who were new to the town, and the four of us went to the flat.

I remember that we had to climb through a window at the back because the front door was locked, but eventually we found ourselves upstairs in a bedroom containing a bed which was almost big enough for four of us.

We polished off the cans and started telling the girls all sorts of weird tales, some of them true, some imaginary. Because they were new to Bryn y Neuadd we told them terrifying stories about some of the patients, how some of them were out of control, threatening and attacking people – none of which were true I hasten to add.

Suddenly Ieu got up and said he was going to the toilet.

He got hold of Dr John, one of the other lads at the party, a big chap, and told him to come up from downstairs pretending that he was off his head in order to scare the girls. Little did Ieu know that Dr John had his chainsaw with him at the party, hoping to get someone there to buy it.

Ieu came back and the stories kept flowing. Suddenly there was a loud knock on the bedroom door and before anyone entered we heard a chainsaw being started. Then the door was kicked open and a wild-looking Dr John came in brandishing the chainsaw.

It scared the life out of the two girls and they dashed down the stairs screaming their heads off, with the three of us laughing at them. We were sorry later, because neither of them as much as looked at us again.

Ieu asked Jonathan what he was doing with a chainsaw at a party and he said that he was hoping to sell it.

'Let me see it working,' said Ieu, 'I could do with a chainsaw.'

They went out and cut down a tree at the back of the flats, but Ieu didn't buy it, it was too dear and better at scaring girls than cutting wood. *The Texas Chainsaw Massacre* was a popular film at that time and I'm sure the girls thought that it was coming true for them that night.

Dic Graiglwyd

Dic was one of those quick-witted men with a ready answer one always remembers. He was a farmer, a farmer who always wore a collar and tie. It's years now since he died, and in 1995 we bought his farm. In those days there was a young man working for us who was forever pulling Dic's leg, and one day he jeered at Dic, who was in his 70s by then, saying that he was too old to get hold of a woman.

'You think you're a hell of a lad, a proper lady killer,' he said, 'You've lost it with the women, Dic, you're much too old.'

'Go home lad and ask your mother,' was the old man's immediate reply.

I was only a boy then but I remember thinking that it was the best reply I had ever heard. One shouldn't always shoot one's mouth off, and Dic Graiglwyd was a crafty old devil.

Jules Hudson

It all began with a phone call from a man named Michael Swift, a television producer working on the programme *Countryfile*. He'd read an article about the ponies and wanted to film an item about them on *Autumn Special* (to be broadcast at the beginning of November 2010) because we rounded them up every autumn.

I agreed, explaining that they were wild ponies and that we herded them on our quad bikes. He understood all that, and that we had three gatherings in a year, this one being the Pencefn one, named after a farm belonging to us.

We had a marvellous day. The man in charge of the film crew was named Jules Hudson, and there was quite a crowd of us on the mountain that day: family and neighbours, all on either two- or four-wheeled bikes. Jules was given a quad bike but lagged behind quite a bit, not being used to the bike or the terrain. We were all shattered at the end of the day; herding ponies takes a lot out of you.

The six-strong film crew were also tired, especially Jules. He intended going home that night but I said: 'Come for a bit of supper with us before you go.'

He readily agreed and said that he was too tired to drive just then anyway.

'No problem,' I said, 'you can eat with us and stay the night.'

So that was that. Supper and a nice bottle of wine, and then he asked where our local pub was. I told him that it was the Llanfair Arms down in the town. He was keen to go there – I suppose he wanted to see how we live in north Wales.

So down we went and into the bar and you couldn't get two such contrasting characters as Jules and Dafydd Ap, the Arms's publican. Dafydd Ap a 70-year-old Welshman, a bit of a rebel in his time, and Jules, the perfect Englishman, well dressed, even for a pony herding, and speaking with a posh English accent.

He ordered a pint for both of us and took out his card.

'What the hell is he doing with that?' asked Dafydd.

And I said, 'He wants to pay for the drinks.'

'Tell him to stuff his card up his arse. We only take cash here, as you know.'

'Put the card in your pocket, Jules,' I said. 'He only takes cash.' I was too much of a coward to give him a literal translation of Dafydd's words.

But he had no cash on him and it cost me a fortune that night to show Jules how north Walians lived! Jules and I are still good friends and we often have a chat on the phone. Who knows, you might see the two of us on another television programme one day!

Not guilty

We're an untidy crowd when we're working, untidy with our clothes, throwing our coats into the Land Rover any old how and grabbing the first one that comes to hand when the need arises. There's no knowing who's wearing what as long as we all have a coat of some description. But this can cause all sorts of bother, as it did for me once.

Dad had taken a load of ewes to Gaerwen one day and after coming home he was sitting in the window of his bungalow and saw me passing on my way to train one of the dogs. He knocked on the window and called me in.

I knew from the way he knocked that there was trouble brewing. So in I went and sat opposite him.

'What's up, Dad?'

'I hope you're behaving yourself,' he said.

'What the hell are you on about?'

'You've been away for a few days.'

'What of it?'

'Did you behave yourself?'

I knew this was serious. I'd never been questioned like this before.

And then it all came out. When he'd arrived at Gaerwen Dad had reached out for his coat in the back of the Land Rover and had put it on. He then went into the café for a bacon butty and a cup of tea. As he was going through his pockets looking for money to pay, a packet of condoms fell out. Realising that it wasn't his coat he assumed it was mine. A group of farmers were standing nearby, saw what happened and began teasing him mercilessly.

'What sort of a coat was it?' I asked.

'A blue one with a logo on the back.'

'That's Uncle Teg's coat,' I said. And Uncle Teg's 74!

Next day couldn't come soon enough for us to tackle him. Mid-morning, when we were having our tea break, Dad asked him point blank: 'What are you doing with a packet of condoms in your pocket, Teg?'

'I've got nothing of the sort,' he answered. 'What would I be doing with such things?'

We all had a go at him, but I was the one who came out of it worst – blamed falsely for playing away, and then accused of putting the condoms in Uncle Teg's pocket. Someone had definitely done it for a lark, but it wasn't me, and we never found out who the culprit was. But the truth will come out, perhaps when the instigator reads this book.

The Pram Race

There is an annual pram race in Llanfairfechan with a different theme to it every year. The race is held on a Sunday, and one Saturday night before the big day, my sister-in-law, Caroline, phoned asking for my help. She was in a team of four or five girls for the competition, and the lad who had promised to push the pram had pulled out at the last minute and they needed a man!

The theme was 'Big Fat Gypsy Wedding', and I had to wear a flat hat, waistcoat, black trousers, white shirt and pumps. There was quite a good turnout, 15 prams in the race and lots of people and children watching. The money raised always goes to charity.

Off we went down to the seashore, to Helen Butler's home where the race was to start. There were Helen, Melinda, Caroline, and Lynne and Jan – two sisters; six in all counting me, and we chose the heaviest girl not the lightest to sit in the pram. We'd had a drink before we started and the girls said that they never tried to win, they only took part for the fun of it.

'Well, I always race to win,' I said, telling the one in the pram to hold on tight. And off we went at such a speed that her legs were up in the air. An element of the race was to have a drink in every pub in Llanfairfechan, finishing at the golf club, and I told the girls to dash to the bar as we arrived at each one and order the drinks. I drank whiskey every time – probably a silly choice – and the girls drank vodka and Coke.

We were ahead of the rest reaching the first pub, and we had two drinks because one of the boys, Pickles, was egging us on. Then on to the sailing club. The girls were supposed to help with the pushing but they kept well back and one of them was struggling. 'I don't do running,' she said! I was pushing and sweating, having by now downed three whiskeys rather quickly and beginning to feel their effect. On we went to the Llanfair Arms on the bridge. Lots of children were running with us and some of them helped me – they were better at pushing than the girls.

There aren't many rules to the race as the object of the event is to raise money, but each team has to pick up something in every pub to have any hope of winning. A ring from one pub, a hair decoration from another and so on, but they all have to be compatible with the day's theme and one object short or unsuitable can cost you the race.

We were at the Llanfair Arms before anyone else but there was no sign of Dafydd behind the bar. We yelled, but he was in the cellar changing the barrels and didn't hear us, and anyway he'd forgotten everything about the race! By the time he appeared three or four of the other teams had also arrived.

Then the steep Penybryn hill faced us. The children had disappeared so there was no help available with the pushing. Caroline tried her best to help me but we were both exhausted and sweating profusely as it was such a fine day. I didn't want another drink but had to drink one quickly before tackling the hill up to the golf club. People were standing outside their houses, shouting and cheering and encouraging the teams as they passed.

We were the first to get to the end and we had to report to the person in charge, Sylvia, and give her all the objects we had collected. But the girls all went straight to the bar and another team finished and went straight to report themselves!

Sylvia came to tell us that we hadn't obeyed the rules and therefore hadn't won. I was flabbergasted, having worked so hard and been so keen to win. But later on when the official announcement was made, they said that we were the winners after all and that really made my day!

Llanffest

A family celebration gave me the idea. Dad has a cousin Mary living in America, whose sons came over to Wales with their families and we held a party for them in the shed at Ty'n Llwyfan, with plenty of food, Welsh bands and so on, and it was a great success. Aunt Falmai and John Ty'n Rhedyn were the ones who kept in touch with them, and they did most of the organising.

Two years later my cousin Megan and Rhian's sister Catherine were celebrating a special birthday and we organised a similar party for them. And that was also a great success.

I was invited to sit on the board of the International Sheep Dogs Society, the Wales chairman was Wyn Edwards, Ruthin, and a friend of mine, Emrys Lewis was the chairman of the Abergele committee of the Society. There were several local branches, all discussing ways to raise money and one evening I volunteered to arrange a rock concert at Ty'n Llwyfan.

The first one, called Llanffest, was in 2007 and we raised £5,000, with part of it going to the sheepdog trials and the rest to local organisations such as the carnival and the football club.

The following year, 2008, we decided to organise a similar event for Tŷ Gobaith (Hope House), the children's hospice, and we offered free camping facilities to those who attended the event. The response was unbelievable; they came from all over and both the camping fields were full. Our lads took care of the stewarding and security and making sure that there was no trouble on the sites. The police did an inspection and they were quite happy with the arrangements.

The concert started with a local group and then we had my wife Rhian, Bryn Fôn, Celt and several other groups. Rhian, being part of the rock scene, knew many of the groups and had no trouble in persuading them to perform. But we had to be quite firm with them all regarding their timing. Each band was allotted a three-quarters-of-an-hour set, but they always want to sing one more song. It was a wonderful evening, everyone enjoying themselves and everyone behaving. Only two youths were marched off by our lads and put on the bus.

A young lad came up to me to say that someone had stolen his brand-new set of drums. Well by then it was dark and there was no chance of searching for them with all the people that were milling around. The fun lasted until two o'clock in the morning.

I got up very early the next day to have a look around. It was very quiet in the first field, the campers still asleep. There was a huge fire in the second field and a group of people sitting around it playing guitars and all sorts of instruments. They'd been at it all night. I asked if they'd seen a drum kit lying around, and one of them said he'd heard drums in the next field during the night. There were only sheep supposed to be there but when I went to look, the drums were there in the middle of the pasture. Someone had taken a fancy to them, had a go at playing them and then done a disappearing act! We never found out who the mysterious drummer was, but I'm sure he enjoyed himself playing to the sheep – and he hadn't damaged the drums in any way.

There was a lot of clearing up to do after the event, especially the shed, but it was all worth it and we raised thousands of pounds for Tŷ Gobaith. We organised several Llanffests after that, with Rhian doing most of the work, but we've stopped doing it by now.

Maybe, sometime in the future, we'll do it again. But nowadays life is too busy and too hard – but not as hard as we let a film crew from London, who came here to produce a television series, believe!

12

School of Hard Knocks

SCHOOL OF HARD Knocks was a television series where a group of youngsters and some older men, who had many problems following abuse of alcohol and drugs, were put through a sort of boot camp in the hope that it would better their circumstances and instil in them a more optimistic attitude to life. One of the producers, Ollie Fraser, had heard of our wild ponies on the Carneddau, and he phoned me to ask if he could bring the group to film them rounding up the herd.

This happened because I'd had a chat with an old friend, John Burns, at 'Mike the Bike's' 50th birthday party. John was friendly with Scott Quinnell, who was in the series, and he had mentioned the ponies to him. He then talked about them with Ollie Fraser and that's how *School of Hard Knocks* came to the Carneddau.

They had chosen the participants at a dole office in Croydon; the youngest was 18 years old and the oldest over 40. Ollie brought them and the film crew up here, complete with Scott Quinnell and Will Greenwood, two ex-rugby players who were an important part of the project.

Ollie told me to take a really hard line with them. I remember his exact words: 'I want you to act in a very positive, stern and scary manner.'

'That's no problem at all,' I said airily.

We arranged everything for the pony roundup on a Saturday, and everyone arrived the night before. Will Greenwood and Scott Quinnell were the first to get here and then the bus bringing the men arrived. They'd had a long and uncomfortable

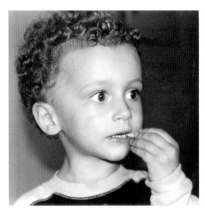

Siôr: he's eaten enough crusts

Siôr as a two year old

Nain Pen with Rolant on her lap (2001)

Rolant (2001)

Day-old Mari (June 2004)

In Horeb chapel vestry – me with Cedric and his shepherd's staff. No echo here!

In the middle of children. Front row: Rolant, Elin Lois, Seren, Ela, Alaw.
Back row: Elin Lloyd, Mari Non, Siôr and me

Disneyland Paris: me, Siôr, Rolant and Mari – with no one lost!

Disneyland Paris: Rolant, Cruella de Vil, Mari, Rhian and Siôr

Renovating the house (2004)

Filming *Cefn Gwlad*: Ieuan, Uncle Huw, Dai Jones, Owen John, Uncle Wil, me, Berwyn and Dad

Sêl gyntaf merlod y Carneddi (2009): Rolant, fi, Mari, Siôr a Dad

The whole family

Huw, Rhian, Sioned and me – the sun was strong!

One of those champagne
moments!

Being conferred mayor of
Llanfairfechan

Farming is a hard life – for farmer and animal

Attending to the feet of the cattle: Dad, Robat, me, Ieuan and Owen John

Dosing the sheep – Owen John (in the background), Robat and me

Dad, Uncle Teg and Uncle Wil. Strange to see them sitting!

Dad, me and Teg

Snowdonia 1890, with my dog, Eryri Cap
Photo: BBC

Wil, my father-in-law, at the Royal Welsh Show in Builth Wells, with Siôr, Rolant and me

Dad celebrating his 60th birthday

Mam, Wil, Dad and Liz (2007)

Rolant, Siôr and Mari (April 2012)

From the mountain to the sea

In my familiar habitat

© Jan Davies

At my work

The 10 who wanted to win the pick-up
Photo: S4C

It was easy to smile at the beginning
Photo: S4C

Me and Mrs J at the James Bond themed *Farmers Weekly* awards

At the Royal Welsh Show after winning the NFU Principality Community Champion award

Photo: *Daily Post*

The Indus team behind the TV series *The Hill Farm*

Photo: BBC Wales

A family picture from *The Hill Farm*

Photo: BBC Wales

At a friend's
wedding, with
the Quinnells

Rhian and me
busy planting

The big snow
of spring 2013
Photo: Ian Lang,
ITV News

journey with no toilet stops and three of them were already drunk before they started out on their trip. When they got to the bottom of the hill, the driver phoned to ask if he could come on up to the farmyard.

I told him there was no way he could manage that as there was a sharp bend between us and the bottom of the road. He would have to leave the bus there and everyone would have to walk up. But he would not listen!

'There'll be no problem,' he said. 'I'll be there now.'

Silly fool! The bus got stuck of course. And we had to hitch it to the big tractor, the John Deere, to free it. And that was no picnic believe me, the chain broke three times and we had to get a stronger one. But we got them up eventually.

Then the director told me, 'You must wear some kind of costume for the filming.' As it happened I had a great big ankle-length wax coat from Australia labelled 'Dry as a bone'. So I put that on and the leather hat I wear around the farm, and grabbed my twelve bore. I'd been hunting rabbits for the crew the night before, I'd bagged ten, but of course they knew nothing of this.

I was told to stand at the far end of a pitch-black shed before the men were led in and the light switched on. What they saw was me standing there in the shadows like an apparition, in the long coat and hat with a gun resting on my shoulder. And the director said, 'This is your farmer.'

You should have seen their faces! There were four white men and the others were all dark skinned with eyes popping out of their heads as I obeyed orders and tried to act the hard man.

'I'm Mr Jones to you,' I said in my loudest voice. 'You're on my farm for three days and you'd better listen to me and do everything I tell you because up here people get lost and die if they step out of line.'

A dramatic pause before continuing: 'Tonight you'll be setting up camp on the mountain, a mile and a half's hard walking from here, so get your gear ready.'

'I've only got pumps,' said a small voice from the back.

'You'll need something better than pumps to climb the mountain,' I said.

'Well, that's all I've got.'

As I mentioned, I'd been shooting rabbits for them and I was told to throw them at them, to hurl them as if I was feeding my dogs. I wasn't too keen to do this, I thought that was going a bit too far, but I was told that shock treatment was the order of the day, that was how they wanted them treated – the good policeman and the bad policeman regime, the kind and the tough, and I was the bad element as they would never see me again. So I threw the rabbits at them. I'd already disembowelled them, but they had to be shown how to skin them. They had no idea what to do, had never seen anything like it, had never seen a rabbit, and had probably never seen a dead animal before.

So off we went up the mountain. It was autumn, pitch dark and pouring with rain. They had small lamps strapped to their heads and some of them took one and a half hours to complete the journey. They were to camp in an old sheep fold belonging to Pencefn, with no tents, only sheets anchored to the walls of the fold to serve as roofs over their heads. It was still raining hard as they struggled to tie the sheets and light a fire to cook the rabbits. They had potatoes and vegetables with them and they were working in groups of four or five.

I told them I was going home to my wife and that I'd see them in the morning. 'At first light,' added Chris, the army instructor, who was with them. No, there was no lie-in for anyone the following day.

I was up there with the film crew by half past six and the poor campers looked terrible. They had hardly slept all night and from what I could gather most of the rabbits had been eaten almost raw – they hadn't a clue how to cook on an open fire.

'Right, boots on and let's go,' I said.

I've never in my life felt so uncomfortable. I was so sorry for them, standing there looking so bedraggled with runny noses, and I having slept all night in my comfortable bed. One of the little dark ones, Pierre, the one in the pumps, was now fitted out with a pair of Wellingtons one of my boys had given him.

Rounding up the ponies was to take place high up on the mountain near Llyn yr Afon, and I told them that they were wild ponies. Then I told them what to do if the animals came towards them threateningly. They were terrified. 'Are there foxes here?' asked one of them, and another asked, 'Are there wolves here?'

I explained that we would chase the ponies in one straight line and asked for the five fittest in their midst to join me to form the line. Will Greenwood and Scott Quinnell volunteered and they also joined the line. Away we went, climbing the steep slopes for about a mile, and by the time we came to the river two of them were worn out and had to rest. Another one was on the phone with his girlfriend. The sound technician said to me in Welsh, 'Listen' and this is what I heard: 'I'm up on this bloody Welsh hill with this bloody mad Welsh farmer. He's going to bloody kill us... If I don't come back... I love you, and if I do come back, I'm never going on these bloody trips again...'

We were halfway up the mountain by now and many in the group were worn out. They'd never walked further than the nearest pub or shop before. Will Greenwood and Scott Quinnell were struggling too, so we sat down to rest. There were still some bilberries left on the mountain and I started eating them.

'What have you got there?' asked Will Greenwood.

'Bilberries,' I said and gave him a handful of the berries mixed with some sheep droppings, and he put them straight in his mouth.

'What on earth?' he choked, spitting them out.

'Sheep shit,' I replied. Everyone laughed at him for being so gullible. Luckily he had a good sense of humour and could take a joke.

He managed to get to the top with us, plus four of the original group, and we had a wonderful round up. We kept the line for about a mile and did as we normally do. The ones that made it to the top enjoyed themselves, they'd never seen anything like it, and it was quite an eye-opener for them. But some of the others had no interest whatsoever in what was going on.

By the time we arrived back I'd made friends with some of them, including Pierre, the lad with the pumps.

'You're not such a hard man after all, are you?' was his comment.

He told me that he was married to a Turkish girl and that they had a little girl, but she and her mother were back in Turkey because he thought that they had a better chance there. He was still in contact with them. He himself was a chef, but he'd lost his job, and where he lived in Croydon he didn't dare venture out after four in the afternoon because of the threat of being attacked. He got up early every morning to do the essentials like shopping. And here was I, opening my door each morning on the beautiful vista of Traeth Lafan and Beaumaris. It made me realise how lucky I am, how privileged I am to live here and do what I do.

When we got back to the farm we had a barbeque on the yard. The group were supposed to spend another night on the mountain, but Will and Scott felt so sorry for them that they booked them into a bunkhouse near Bangor, but they knew nothing of that.

In the evening we took them to the Bangor Rugby Club where Clive Griffiths, who used to train the Welsh rugby squad, gave them a talk and showed them a film about Joe Calzage, Nigel Benn and others. Then they had an intensive training session with him before going for a pint and a good night's rest in the bunkhouse. The theory of the good policeman and the bad policeman had been put to the test, and by the end you felt that they had learnt something from their experience.

When I saw the programme I realised what the producers had in mind. I think four or five of the group managed to find work eventually because they'd been trained by people who had seen their potential and had been able to offer them jobs.

It was quite a special experience for me to be part of such a project and to meet people like Will Greenwood and Scott Quinnell. Not everyone can say that they've had those two in their kitchen drinking tea and eating biscuits. Enough of that, or I'll be accused of name dropping!

But we have forged a link. The Quinnell family come up here to stay in one of my brother's holiday cottages, and Rhian and I and the children have stayed with Nicola and Scott and their kids in south Wales. They are very good friends of ours by now.

13

Various Topics

Tagging

ONE MORNING WHEN I happened to be on Anglesey, I heard Richard Parry Hughes speaking on the radio. He was saying that farmers shouldn't be old-fashioned and keep looking back all the time, and I felt that he was talking us down as an industry because of our attitude to electronic identification – tagging with microchips.

We had been using these for about five years, and I didn't regard them as efficient. I arrived home from Anglesey feeling that this man shouldn't be allowed to get away with it, saying what he did, so I e-mailed Dylan Jones, the programme's presenter. I had been in touch with him many times, having been on his programme *Taro'r Post* arguing against these tags and explaining their shortcomings. Mia, his researcher replied asking if I would be willing to go on air to voice my objections.

I had a call from Rhys Owen, head of agriculture at the Snowdonia National Park that morning, and I mentioned to him that I'd heard Richard Parry Hughes on the radio and that I'd contacted Dylan Jones and would be on the his programme at lunchtime to respond to his criticism of farmers.

'Jones,' he said to me, 'you've made a hell of a mistake. Do you know who he is?'

'No,' I said, 'but he was talking through his hat.'

'Well, he's been the leader of Gwynedd County Council, and

he's not a man to be taken lightly. You'll catch it this lunchtime. You've really gone overboard this time.'

I didn't believe I had, I knew I was right because I'd had experience of these tags, yet I felt a bit shaken because of what Rhys had said. He knows me well and for him to say what he did, this man must be a pretty strong character, a public speaker, and at the end of the day I'm just an ordinary farmer.

I can't say that I was nervous, but I think there was a quiver in my voice when I went on the programme that day.

In my opinion the interview went quite well. At first I showed respect to the man, just as I have been taught, letting him air his views because he was older than me. But then he became quite critical and started talking me down. And I thought hold on a minute, I'm not going to take this lying down, and I was beginning to get a bit agitated, and Dylan, as usual, was stirring it as he does in order to get a good argument going, and I wasn't very clear who was saying what, Richard Parry Hughes or Dylan, because I was so worked up.

Hughes was trying to retract, suggesting it was a joke. Then he changed his argument and said that big lorries were passing my farm carrying lambs from Scotland to the Welsh Country Foods slaughterhouse in Gaerwen. I don't know why he said this, unless he was suggesting that our lambs, which we farmed nearby, weren't good enough. When he said this I knew I'd got him, because this had nothing to do with what we were arguing about. So I kept at him and suggested that he should wake up and smell the coffee!

After the interview people phoned me to thank me for my stand, and I had a positive response from farmers when I next went to market. Following that interview a Welsh TV programme, *Y Byd ar Bedwar* (The World on Four), contacted me, and Eifion Glyn made a programme about the microchips.

I feel that through these programmes I've had the opportunity to present the farmers' side of the argument.

But it didn't work. Nobody listened. We are still in the same situation, in the same boat. This electronic tagging does not work and the farmers of Wales know that. We have no central database to control it properly; it all depends on what is done and recorded on the farm, and the chips and tags come loose from the animals and are lost. Perhaps it could work in a shed, but it does not work on mountains like the Carneddau.

This is a European ruling and I believe the Assembly Government is against it. Elin Jones was against it when she was Minister of Agriculture, but her hands were tied, and she could do nothing because of the European ruling, as the United Kingdom is part of the European Union. Most of the continent's farms are small, and maybe it works there. Fifty sheep on a farm in France is one thing, thousands on the hills of Wales is another matter!

I haven't heard from Richard Parry Hughes since the programme; maybe I will after the publication of this book. Perhaps we could meet over a cup of tea – or a pint.

Miami

Four of us went for a few days to Miami – Rhian and her sister Catherine, me and a friend of mine, Mark Hughes. We went on a Fly Drive holiday with one of the holiday companies, flying to Fort Lauderdale and hiring a car there. It was a four-hour journey to Miami, the car was a big American saloon and the roads were good. We were doing good time and speeding along.

Mark was hungry, so we stopped for breakfast at a café and to have a look around for an hour or so. Everyone who goes to America receives a ticket for tolls because you have to pay for using the motorways. An American at the café told us that we were lucky that we had stopped because the ticket would show the police that we had been speeding, and we would have received a fine for over speeding and travelling too long without stopping, although we had not seen a policeman anywhere.

We arrived at our hotel in Miami and it wasn't far from the downtown area of the city, so we decided to go and have a look at the place. Mark studied the map and I drove, although we had no idea where to go. Rhian saw a sign advertising a free concert starring the famous Aerosmith group, and so we decided to look for the venue of the concert. The receptionist at the hotel had warned us against going to some areas, because people there would know that we were driving a hired car and we'd be in danger of being mugged. But the concert was too much of a temptation.

I have never seen so many roads in all my life, each one consisting of five or six lanes. There weren't many cars about and we were in a very poor district. We came to traffic lights and had to stop. At once a man approached us: 'Can I do your windows, man?'

Rhian and Catherine in the back urged us to ignore him, but perhaps he would have smashed the window, so we agreed. He washed the front window before the lights changed. I gave him two dollars and on we went. We came to another set of lights and had to stop. Another man stepped out and asked: 'Can I do your windows, man?' I said that we'd already had them done. 'I'll do the back ones for you,' he said and I parted with another two dollars. I came to yet another set of lights, and yet another man stepped out, but I told him at once that all our windows had been cleaned and we drove through the lights fearing that he would be angry. I must admit that I had panicked a bit because there was quite a sinister atmosphere about the place, a feeling of threatening expectancy, and although we were in a car we were very aware of it.

We arrived unscathed back at the hotel without finding the concert venue and the receptionist asked us where we had been. We told him. 'Jesus,' he said, 'where you've been they'd shoot you for three dollars!'

Later on that evening we were sitting in the hotel lounge and details of the free concert we had been looking for appeared on the screen, together with the names of everyone taking part, and pictures of the thousands of people who had flocked to it.

Sheepdog Trials

The organisation of sheepdog trials in Wales includes a points system whereby competitors who take part in the Welsh national championship can be selected for the international competition between the home nations.

In 2006 I acquired enough points to take part in the national event which was held that year in Cardiff.

A friend of my father's, Wyn Gruffydd, attended every year and he booked two nights for himself, my father and me. We were staying at different bed and breakfast establishments belonging to the same owner.

It transpired that I was with the Pentrefoelas contingent, and was sharing a room with Alwyn Williams (Corrach), who had been in the Welsh team, and another friend, Carl, from Blaenau Ffestiniog.

After attending the trials in the afternoon we all went to a tavern for a meal that evening. There was much leg pulling there and one of the lads asked me if I knew that Corrach was a terrible snorer. I didn't of course, but thought since he knew that I was sharing a room with him, that they might be having me on.

There were two beds in the room, one for me and one for Corrach, with Carl sleeping on a mattress on the floor. Every apartment was chock-a-block because of the trials.

As soon as he hit the canvas Corrach started snoring and I thought he was teasing me. Nothing of the sort. I needed a good night's sleep because I would be performing with my dog in the morning, but I didn't sleep a wink in my bed that night. I have never heard such a din. Even the wall was shaking.

Carl slept immediately, being probably used to the situation, but I couldn't. I lay on my bed for an hour, shouting at him at times and even getting up to shake the bed. But to no avail and in the end I got up and took the bed clothes with me to the parlour where I tried to sleep on the sofa. But I could still hear the snoring.

I slept for three or four hours before a sudden noise woke me up and I wasn't sure what was happening, but the next minute the door opened and the landlady stood there, and when she saw me she let out a loud scream. I flung the bedclothes back and stood up. I never wear pyjamas in bed, only my underpants, and when she saw me like this she let out an even louder scream.

'Were you snoring?' she asked.

'Snoring?' I said. 'Listen.'

And the sound of snoring came from the room where Corrach was sleeping.

Things didn't go well in the trials. I made a bit of a mess, to be honest. I could blame lack of sleep for my poor showing, but I don't think I would have performed any better had I had a good night's sleep. There will be further opportunities hopefully, but although he was a smashing lad, I will not be sharing the same boarding house, let alone the same room, as Corrach again!

Hernia

A most painful and horrid affliction! And I well remember how I got it. We have a pasture on the mountain called Ffridd Pen Cefn Crwn, a perfectly oval field, and we used to have cattle there at one time. A calf got stuck there and I went to try to free it myself, a silly thing to do because he was a big strong calf. Whilst struggling with it, I felt a sudden stab of pain low down in my abdomen, a most dreadful pain as if someone had stuck a knife into me. There was a little lump there and I thought I had strained a muscle and that it would get better in time. Rhian tried to persuade me to got to the doctor, but I kept refusing, thinking it would heal itself. But it didn't, it grew bigger and bigger and in the end I had to give in, although it was a busy time on the farm, what with lambing and harvesting the silage.

The doctor told me that I had a hernia and would have to wait at least six months before receiving treatment. But he suggested that I should have a private consultation at the North Wales Health Centre, paying £200, and maybe having the treatment quicker than on the National Health.

The consultant agreed to perform the operation in November when things were quiet on the farm. There were three others on the ward with me, three who were older than me, in their 60s, and we were all treated on the same day, starting with the eldest, and ending with me. That evening Rhian and her mother came to see me, but I didn't see them. The man in the next bed saw them however, and got the fright of his life, ending up shouting all over the place. Both had earlier been to a funeral, and all he saw were two women in long black coats, wearing red lipstick staring down at him. He thought they were vampires and, when there is a need to, I still remind them both of the man's impression of them!

Come Dine with Me

Spring 2013: we had just finished lambing and were sitting at the table finishing our dinner when a friend of mine from Channel 4, Paula West, phoned and asked if I knew that they were filming one programme of the series *Come Dine with Me* in north Wales and did I fancy it? The deadline for showing an interest was the end of the day. I'm not much of a cook really – Rhian is the expert – but I decided there and then to go for it. So I tweeted my reply and immediately there was a tweet back to confirm, and that's how it started.

I gave them my phone number and was called by a lady, Jess

Suckling, and she and a colleague came up to interview me filming with a small camera. Over a 160 people had applied, they whittled the number down to ten, filmed the ten, and took the film to Channel 4 where someone selected four from the ten. Having done quite a bit of TV work I had a good idea of what they wanted, so I sold myself as a farmer, as a food producer and as someone who would be there to entertain them as a cook! I thought it would be an opportunity to have some fun, to reveal another side to me, and of course to display my prize leg of lamb! It worked because I was selected as one of the four.

A taxi picked me up to go to there but, when I arrived, Jess Suckling, said to me: 'You can't wear that shirt. Has nobody told you? It will strobe. Leave it to me.' So she went into this person's house, and soon came out with a blue shirt. I changed quickly in the garden with everybody looking on, and then we went into the house. I knocked on the door, bottle of wine in hand. It was Dale's house in Gaerwen, the first of the four and the first to cook a meal for us, and we were going to eat Thai fish cakes, something I wasn't too keen on. As I had said when filming for the part, I don't like bum burning food!

We were warmly welcomed and I met the other three: Roxanne, a very glamorous and good-looking young woman, Dale himself, who was very pleasant, and Catrin, a teacher who was like me, Welsh speaking.

I thought it a great opportunity to do some advertising so when Dale asked me what I wanted to drink I asked for a glass of milk, and every night, in the four houses visited, I had a glass of milk before we started. After that, of course, the wine was flowing. Dale had prepared a Thai theme for us and the main course was Thai fish cakes, which were quite hot. Indeed the whole meal was quite hot. Catrin and I got on like a house on fire, probably because we were both Welsh speaking, and we found it quite difficult to talk to each other in English. And on this first night Roxanne said quite abruptly: 'Speak f***ing

English!' Cheeky! She came from Colwyn Bay! Catrin kept whispering: 'I know you', having probably seen me on TV!

The format of the programme was that each of us prepared a meal in our own homes, and the three who weren't cooking gave marks to the fourth every time. So after eating we went out to the taxis to decide on our marks. I gave Dale seven.

It was an enjoyable evening. We all had probably too much to drink, but I was in my element, always a bit flirtatious when there are young women about, and there were two of them! Well, when you're doing a TV programme and you're going home by taxi, you've got to relax!

The second night we were at Roxanne's house in Colwyn Bay where we had a very warm welcome and a nice meal with food from different continents: margarita, frankfurter sausages, beef Wellington – Mexican, German, and English. She really went out of her way to make us welcome and to dine us well, the beef Wellington was fantastic. Then we had the entertainment, a piniata with every one blindfolded. I gave Roxanne eight that night because I thought that her evening was better than Dale's.

On the third night we were in Catrin's home in Tregarth. It was a lovely place and we had a fantastic welcome. The food was very good too, not quite as good as Roxanne's, perhaps. We had lamb, which was a very good choice, but I like my lamb well cooked, and it was a bit pink for me. After the meal we had a delightful surprise. A choir had turned up, a male voice choir, Hogia'r Ddwylan, a party which drew its members from both sides of the Menai Straits, and it was really excellent. I felt the hairs on my back standing on end whilst I listened to them. I knew some of the members and, as I was standing near Roxanne listening to them, some of the members came up afterwards to ask who she was. There was a bit of nudge nudge (wink wink), in their greetings. Catrin's boyfriend was the choir's conductor, and she had arranged for them to come to sing without their knowing what the occasion was. Although she was very good, Catrin was given seven by me because Roxanne, to my mind, was better.

And then, on the fourth and final night, it was the turn of Mr Jones! The arrangement was for the film crew to arrive at ten o'clock in the morning, and they were going to spend the whole day filming, but as a farmer I couldn't spend the whole day with them.

When the time for cooking came I started with pea and pancetta soup, made with home-grown peas, indeed as many as possible of the ingredients for the meal were home-grown. The lamb I was cooking was put in the Rayburn and then I had to go out to get the eggs for the dessert and the camera crew followed me – they were an excellent crowd of people. When a ewe bolted from the yard without its lamb, I had to chase the lamb and again the camera crew followed. It was all part of the whole scene.

So when the evening came, Rhian wasn't allowed in the house and she and the children had to collect their things and go down to my parents' bungalow, and the children had to swear to secrecy that their father was being filmed for *Come Dine with Me.* But later in the evening they and their mother sneaked back into the house, to the lounge to listen, and had a giggle as they heard me going on and on entertaining my guests. According to Rhian I was really on a roll, although they couldn't quite understand what I was saying.

But there you are. When people come to your house you've got to welcome and entertain them. I gave them all a signed copy of my Welsh autobiography and they all had a glass of milk. I thought that the food was fantastic considering that I cooked it. The lamb was beautiful but I was a bit disappointed to see Roxanne picking what she said were bits of bone from the meat. I have every faith in the butcher who slaughters our lambs and I have never seen any trace of bone in the meat. But it was part of the whole set-up, and at the end of the day Roxanne was the best cook of the four participants, and she deserved to win.

I really enjoyed it all; it was an experience that I will recall with fond memories. I'm still friends with Catrin, and we met up with Dale at the Anglesey Arms some time ago. Life is too short to hold grudges, and it was a good promotion for farmers and for Welsh produce. When I go to speak to societies, the first thing asked when it's time for questions is, 'How did you enjoy *Come Dine with Me?'* That's proof that many people watched it, and many people enjoyed it. Some people ask me if Rhian helped me with the cooking. But there was no help – no help was allowed; I had to do it all myself! It was a good promotion for home produce; even Roxanne brought a pint of milk with her on the last night!

I never cook and I had never made a pudding before. I practised making the ice cream once, in the previous week – that was all. I did tell them there was a special ingredient in the ice cream, bull semen, and that remark was included in the programme and drew a lot of attention from those who saw it and from the press. I hasten to add that it was only a joke, lest someone really believed me!

Catrin said that she had never held a lamb in her arms, so we brought one in for her, and she said that stroking it was like stroking a cat. Some people criticised us for showing two sides to the business, the pretty cuddly live lamb, and then eating lamb for our meal. But that's life and that's reality.

It was the last night and at the end we had a party. Rhian sang with the band and we all enjoyed ourselves. The result of the competition was revealed: Dale had fourth place, Catrin and I were joint second, and Roxanne won. It was a fair result, and she was absolutely ecstatic. We had a very good time, including enjoying Dale's party trick – pulling out his false tooth. There was some lamb left over and I made lamb baps for the film crew, and they really enjoyed them – I was a salesman to the death! It was two o'clock in the morning by the time everything was finished and the camera crew had left. We cleared up and washed the dishes in the dishwasher because Rhian didn't want to face them in the morning. We made friends for life during the programme and it was all worthwhile.

14

Adjudicating

It all began with a phone call – what else! It's remarkable how many of my experiences have begun with a phone call. The caller was a man named Ben, asking me if I would be interested in going to Manchester for an interview, because they were looking for judges for the programme *BBC Young Farmer of the Year*, a programme in the series *Young Talent*.

I had a bit of a shock to be honest, that they were asking me, but he said that they were contacting quite a few people because they needed a certain number for the interviews. So I decided to take the day off from farm work, and that at the expense of the BBC – what could be better!

The interview was held at the new BBC centre not far from the Lowry in Salford. It's a huge new complex near the end of the Manchester Ship Canal. There were half a dozen large buildings there and I had to phone to find the right one, a building that housed studios and offices, and home to programmes such as *Blue Peter* and *Dragons' Den*.

I had to go through the security rigmarole before being led to an office and meeting a man named Curtis, the show's producer and wore make-up and a false tan. He was a very pleasant man. He went out to fetch me a cup of coffee, leaving me on my own. On the desk there was a pile of papers, and I started poking around and found the names of people to be interviewed – people like Adam Henson from the programme *Countryfile*, and the farm manager of the Duke of Westminster's estate. And when I saw the list I decided that I hadn't a hope in hell of getting the job.

Curtis came back with the coffee with Ben, the chief cameraman, in tow, and they both started asking me questions about what I did on the farm and general questions of that nature. I believed the interview had gone quite well, and before I left Curtis suggested that it would be a good idea if I met Dorian, the working producer of the programme, as I had travelled such a distance for my interview.

Dorian was very chatty, and after I'd shaken hands with him he said, 'I've not had my hand shaken like that in years!' He was a very kind and considerate person and he walked with me from the building, thanked me for coming so far and said that I had made a good impression on Curtis and Ben in the interview and that I would know my fate within a week or two.

After a fortnight had gone by I received a telephone call offering me the job, and I accepted. Then dates were organised; filming would take me away from home for four days, but before that I had to visit Manchester again. 100 young farmers had applied for the competition, but they had been reduced to 20. My first task therefore, as an adjudicator, with the other judge, David Finkle, whom I had never met, was to reduce the 20 to four for the programme.

I received the particulars of the 20 beforehand and they were obviously a good bunch, between 16 and 25 years old, boys and girls. Dave and I had to interview them and give them tasks to complete: a quiz about various aspects of farming, a number of farm tools and implements to identify, such as a calf-pulling instrument and various other things. For some reason or another, they seemed to be afraid of me, perhaps because I have a big loud voice, but they had good answers. They were 20 very special people and it was difficult to decide on the four to appear on the programme.

One or two were very quiet and the television people noted that, but Dave and I insisted that we were looking for the best farmer, not a television star, and we had our way.

Having considered all aspects we decided on the four:

Seth Blakey, 18, from Clitheroe; Rhys Lewis, 24, from Neath; William Alec Ives, 19, from Buckinghamshire, and one girl, Robynne Strawbridge, 21, from Devon. Seth worked on a farm and went out shearing, Rhys was a very pleasant young man, and William was short and stocky but full of himself. We called Robynne a feisty female, a bit of a character, a strong personality, giving the sort of answers television people like.

Then we chose one as a stand-by, who wasn't used, but came with us to Suffolk for the four days filming.

Those who hadn't been selected were naturally very disappointed, and I was asked to have a word with them. I told them how good they were, that they had been selected from 100 other applicants, and that they could be proud of themselves. I expected Dave Finkle to strike a similar tone, but what he did was to complain about the low standard and that he was disappointed, and that didn't go down very well with them!

Suffolk was a long drive from Llanfairfechan. I started out at 8.30 a.m. and arrived at 4 p.m. Half an hour before arriving I received a telephone call from Curtis saying that he would wait for me in the hotel in order to go over the script. Script I thought, what script! I have never spoken from a script and I was beginning to feel sorry that I had agreed to do the job.

However, I arrived safely and met Curtis and some other chap from the BBC, and found out quite soon that the script was nothing more than a list of declarations to be recited at the beginning of the programme, at most lasting a few seconds, things like: 'I believe that the best farmer should be able to...' Sentences like that, not a whole script for all the proceedings, as I had feared. But I don't know whether it was fatigue or lack of experience using scripts, but I had the Dickens of a job learning those few sentences. I met the programme's presenter, George Lamb, and he was very pleasant and over a pint or two he went through the script with me so that I felt better about things. Then I received a telephone call from Curtis saying that a taxi would pick me up at 8 a.m. the following morning, and so I had an extra pint or two because I didn't have to drive the next day, but I was in bed by ten, tired out after a long day.

The following day, after a good breakfast where everything you could think of was on offer, I went to the studio and got the fright of my life when I arrived there. Everything was to be filmed in an enormous hanger-like building, and there were about 50 BBC people milling around: secretaries, sound and lighting and camera crews. Nothing like *Fferm Ffactor* or *Snowdonia 1890*. In those programmes I was in my comfort zone, but not here, where everything was different. I was far from home and in an unfamiliar situation and feeling most uncomfortable.

The first item on the agenda was to record the declarations in the script, the 'takes' as they called them, before the competitors arrived. Dave Finkley had been Jimmy Doherty's farm manager and had been seen fairly recently on the programme *Jimmy's Farm*. By now he was more of a television presenter than anything else, and although he had been a lecturer at agricultural colleges before taking up TV work, he wasn't as hands-on as I am. You could say that I was the rough and he was the smooth.

Then I was introduced to Chesney, my runner for the four days. I had no idea what a runner was, but it was explained to me that whatever I wanted, even a cup of tea, I only had to ask Chesney, and I thought, good Lord, if I want a cup of tea, I can fetch it myself. But that's the sort of world it is, a strange world for me, and quite different to television in Wales too, I should think.

We went out of the hanger to sit on two chairs to make our declarations of what we expected to see and the characteristics of a good farmer. Thankfully Dave offered to go first, but I think we filmed this part at least 20 times. I couldn't for the life of me say the right things. I just went blank every time and I have never felt so sick in my life. They had spent a lot of money on me and I kept asking myself if I had taken on more than I could cope with. It wasn't the adjudicating that worried me, I was quite happy with that – the bloody script was the problem!

I have done a lot of television, but had never felt like this. Turn tail and go home, that is how I felt. Anyway George Lamb arrived and asked, 'What's the problem Jones?' and I answered, 'I can't get these bloody lines into my head.' Then Curtis and one or two others arrived and that made me feel worse.

I told them that Welsh was my first language and George said that I didn't have to say exactly what was in the script. 'Get the key words in, that's all,' he said and I could say what had to be said in my own words. And once I was allowed to forget the script, everything was fine.

The whole episode took about an hour, before we started on the competition itself.

The first competition for the four was to dose five sheep, treat their feet and shear them, and because I was the sheep farmer, Dave told me to take the lead in this competition and he would do the same in the next.

To perform these tasks under pressure was quite an ordeal for the young competitors, and of course they were making mistakes, forgetting to strap the doses which meant that they only had one hand free to dose, things like that. Then came the shearing and they were doing it two by two, starting with Seth and William, then Robynne and Rhys.

Seth was completely professional, having had plenty of experience going out contracting during the season, but it was a new experience for William, and he had difficult sheep to shear – Dorsets covered with fleece like teddy bears. It was a hell of a job to shear them and all five had to be finished within the allotted time.

William hadn't a clue. He lost the plot completely, going from one part of the sheep to the other rather than shearing tidily in an orderly fashion. Then the next minute he clipped the end part of one of the sheep's teats. I had told them that I would put a stop to things if I saw something that I wasn't happy with, and so everything had to be stopped because there was blood all over the place and, filming or not, the well-being of the sheep was the most important consideration. Of course they were filming throughout the shearing and the tension was unbearable, making everything worse. The vet came then to treat the sheep, and Seth was allowed to carry on and finish because his shearing was excellent.

The sheep owner was there making things awkward for us judges and the competitors, but she came to thank me for putting a stop to things when the sheep was injured.

Seth finished four of the sheep but his time was up before he could get to grips with the fifth. But he had done quite a good job on the other four.

It was then the turn of Robynne and Rhys. Neither had sheared a sheep before but both knew how to use the machine and off they went. Rhys made a pretty good attempt at it but he left the back legs and the heads unsheared. The sheep looked like lions! Robynne started well, with the back legs, but she was soon without a plan and like William jumping from one place to the other. She had no idea and I was in two minds what to do because there was so much tension there. But I winked at the producer, leant forward to switch off the machine whilst telling Robynne that I had to do it because she had no idea what she was doing.

Then the tears flowed, she was breaking her heart and I thought, Oh dear me, what have I done now! I had been quite hard on them – it was expected of me, and in any case there is nothing nice and fancy about farming, it is a hard business and you can't go on breaking down and crying every time something goes wrong. You could be crying every day. But there we are, it was a difficult situation, filming taking place with everybody looking at her, she had never been in such a situation before, doing something she had never done previously.

I went to her and had a word in her ear, and she composed herself. Fair play to Rhys, his sheep looked a hell of a sight, but at least he finished the task.

The first task had been completed and everybody went out of the shed while Dave and I retired to a little hut to discuss the competitors. The expulsion system used was the same as that for *Fferm Ffactor*. We had decided that no one would be asked to leave after the first task, but they didn't know that.

Then we went out and I wanted to go to the toilet. One of the lads told me to go right round the back of the building, otherwise I would have to face the families. We didn't know this at the time, but all the families were present, mothers and fathers, sisters and brothers, but we were being kept far enough away from them.

It was quite a distance to go round and I thought that I had nothing to be afraid of, so out I went through the steel door and towards the toilets. It was a fine day and the families were standing around talking to each other as I walked through them to the toilet. I have never received so many dirty looks in my life as I had that morning. Without our knowledge, they had heard on the monitors in the studio or cutting room everything that we as judges had been saying while their children were busy with their task, and we had been saying quite harsh things. I remember in particular Rhys's mother looking at me, and if looks could kill I would have been stone dead. That's why I was advised to take the long way round to the toilet, and that's what I did on the way back!

I hadn't realised it at the time, but the response of the parents to what we were saying was part of the programme. They were filming the families watching us and reacting to our judgments.

I told Curtis what had happened and he laughed and said, 'Do you know what they are calling you? The Welsh bastard!' I felt terrible. I've been called a few names in my time but never a Welsh bastard. But when all was said and done, the BBC had asked me to be there to judge, not make friends.

We then went to the exclusion ceremony. Each competitor came to stand before us and we told them how disappointed we had been and that they needed to think more carefully about what they were doing. We then told them that one should be leaving the competition but that we had decided to keep them all in for the time being. George, the presenter, asked us who we would have excluded, and I answered 'William,' because he had cut the sheep's teat. William gave me quite a look, as if he was saying, who does he think he is? He was a bit of a lad and felt confident that he would win. But he would have deserved to go whatever the girl Robynne had done. She made a mess of things but she didn't cut the sheep, and that was worse than anything else that could have happened. Dave agreed, and that didn't please William either.

All tasks were condensed into a one-hour programme and each challenge followed the other as if they had all been filmed in one day, but that wasn't the case.

On the second day was the pigs' challenge, featuring 15 pigs with us the judges selecting the best five for breeding. The competitors had to do the same and William chose the same five as us, and answered every question we asked him. He was spot on with each one. Robynne was the next and she also did well. Indeed the four had improved, there was less tension in the air and it was an easier task than shearing. We judges were also more relaxed, and had talked to the four after the first day to encourage them and remind them that they were ambassadors for farming.

But we had to select one that would be leaving the competition. It would have been difficult after the task of judging the pigs, but the next task was loading the 15 pigs into a trailer, driving them to the ring, backing the tractor and trailer, placing gates on either side, and unloading them.

William went first and he used his brains, putting straw on the floor of the trailer and the ramp to make a stage for the animals to walk on, and the pigs went in immediately. It was Robynne's turn next, and she did the same, but did not remove the straw from the ramp after loading, and the back could not shut properly as there was straw still there. Rhys did well too, and so did Seth, although he was a little bit rough and ready. Indeed everyone did well, much better than the previous day, but for me William stood out. He had put the trouble with the shearing behind him, and he was excellent.

We went to the hut to discuss and decide who had to go. We both agreed that William was the best on the day, but the previous day had to be taken into account as well. We both agreed that Robynne was the worst of the four. She had done fairly well on the first day, before making a mess of the shearing and crying. I felt that had she grabbed the machine after I had stopped it and said that she was going to continue, she would have won points. But she didn't. She had broken her heart and that is what made the difference, and the fact also that William had selected the same five pigs as us, and he was the only one to do that.

Then to the expulsion. I knew by now how Dai Jones and Wynne Jones felt in *Fferm Ffactor*. But we announced that Robynne had to go. I honestly felt for her, but we had to be fair to the other competitors.

The next task was a quiz, one competitor at a time, with both of us asking the questions. Not unlike my experience on *Fferm Ffactor*, with a chair in the middle and us standing on either side with strong lights and strobes everywhere. We asked alternate questions and if they were answered incorrectly, there was plenty of time to ask them why they'd offered that particular answer.

Well, the pressure got to the three in this task, and this happend when I, not Dave, was asking the questions. Me, the Welsh bastard! I wonder why? However it was close between them. I felt that Rhys had performed well enough to go to the final, to be one of the final two; he had not been great but he had been steady. We called him 'Steady Eddie'. So it was between Seth and William for the high jump. Seth was only 18 and he lost his way completely with the questions. It was a close call but when we asked William how he saw farming, he gave an excellent answer, whilst Seth did nothing except talk about his flock of sheep. He couldn't see further than that, he failed to recognise the influence he would have if he won the competition, the influence on other young farmers throughout Britain. For me, he wasn't mature enough to be a winner.

So we announced that Seth had to go, and he took it very well. I went to him and shook his hand and I saw that his mother was outside. I went round the back so that I didn't have to meet her but, as I turned the corner, we came face to face and she shouted, 'Can I have a word?' I thought I was going to get a bollocking. Dave had disappeared into the toilet and I had no choice but to face her and this is what she said:

'I'd like to thank you.'

'What for?' I asked.

'Well, I think you've been very fair. I thought you were very hard in the first challenge, but you've been very honest and very fair.'

I thanked her and said why I thought that he wasn't good enough to go through to the final, and she said that she completely agreed with me.

Well, I felt better after that, because there is nothing worse than a mother with her child, like an old hen, after you because you've done something to her offspring!

I happened to see Rhys afterwards and he was crying his eyes out, with his sweetheart trying to console him. Crying although he was still in the competition! Yes, it was a hard and emotional time for everybody, and I was glad to return to the hotel in the taxi and that night I was in bed by half past nine, dead tired.

The final challenge on the morrow was at Joe's farm. Joe was a cattle-dealer and we had met before filming started. Only Rhys and William were left and this was quite a challenge for them, but a challenge that would demonstrate clearly who was the better farmer of the two.

They had to pair five cows with five calves and we had tricked them by including one calf that didn't belong to any of the cows and, fair play, William saw the trick at once and that gained him good marks.

The next task was to fetch and set up moving pens to keep the cows in, working together as a team and then as individuals to get them into a crush. Each cow and calf had to be put into a crush, where the animal is enclosed in a confined space, and then a yoke is placed under its neck to lift its head up. Getting them into a crush was a difficult task, and we both watched every move carefully, and observed their attitude towards the animals when things became difficult. Then they had to put thermometers in the animals' back sides to take their temperature, and dose them if necessary. It was easy to get confused when recording the details of all the cows as they went through, but I noticed that Rhys had recorded the number of each animal carefully. William didn't and that created confusion later on, but he admitted his failure.

Some of the animals were restless and difficult to control, but Rhys was quiet and patient with them, and William more aggressive. He fixed the yoke too tightly round one calf's neck until it fainted and the vet had to attend to it. This was a significant error.

After finishing with the cows, the pens had to be loaded back on the trailer, strapped in and taken back to the bottom of the field.

William had quite a high opinion of himself as I said earlier. He kept saying, 'Call me William the winner.'

After all the tasks had been completed, we had to decide on the winner. Dave inclined towards William, the confident one, whilst I favoured Rhys, the more stable and quiet of the two. We asked the two men, who were running the farm, which they would choose, and one said William and the other Rhys, and it developed into quite an argument between them, so that was no help to us!

But as we went at it seriously to decide, analysing all the tasks they had undertaken, I had to draw Dave's attention to the bad error William had made when the yoke was fixed too tightly on one calf, an error which could have resulted in the death of the calf. And Dave admitted that William had been insolent with him and had asked him, 'What do you know about farming? You're just a lecturer.' There was final agreement therefore that Rhys was the winner.

Those responsible for filming the programme couldn't wait, they were at us all the time wanting to know the outcome of the competition, while we took our time in order to arrive at the right decision. Then, when the time came, Dave spoke for William, emphasising his strengths, while I did the same for Rhys before George, the presenter, announced that Rhys was the winner.

Rhys's family came to thank us and his mother said that Rhys was a good lad, having lost his father three years previously, and running the farm himself. I was happy to think that winning the competition would be a boost to his career, helping him realise that he was on the right track. And William's attitude in the end was also good, as if he'd grown up during the competition.

The television producer was more than happy, saying that they had material for a good programme, one of the best in the series. Maybe you saw it on television in February 2012.

I was tired and ready for bed so that I could make an early start for home the next day. I must admit that I was missing my family, we are a close-knit unit and none of us likes to be far away from the others. It had been a long four days.

But when I had a pint with George and Sam back at the hotel, they said that they were going to a party. One of the girls was 30 and a party had been arranged unbeknown to her in a large house outside the village where most of the TV people stayed.

So off we went and we ate our fill. There was plenty of food there. During the evening I had a chat with the one who was responsible for filming the reactions of the families to the tasks and to our comments, and she said how pleased Rhys's family was that he had won. I said that he thoroughly deserved it.

She then said that the families absolutely hated me at first, but that they had more respect for me by the end and that the words 'Welsh bastard' had disappeared. They regarded me as a farmer who knew the ropes, rather than one who likes to talk about farming, like lecturers in a college. I would like to work with Dave Finkle again one day.

Yes, I was dead tired that night and had no urge to go to a party, but I'm glad that I did, if only to know that I had done a decent job.

It was a lovely feeling to head back to north Wales and home to Rhian and the children. I really enjoy going away, and I am always on the go, but it is at home with family and acquaintances that I feel happiest, and the best thing about wandering is returning home to Ty'n Llwyfan.

15

Finally...

BRINGING TO MIND memorable events and happenings for this book has awoken many mixed feelings in me, and has made me realise how varied and changeable life is, like the weather on the Carneddau, fine and stormy, warm and cold, kind and threatening, and one week in particular comes to mind immediately as I ponder these things.

It was the first week of August 1997, and the National Eisteddfod was held at Bala. The best eisteddfod ever for me, the location perfect, the weather fine, and Rhian singing with the group Family Dog in the competition for rock groups. The adjudicator was Siân James and there were two winners, Rhian's group and Fuzzy Duck from Blaenau Ffestiniog.

We had a great weekend, a good crowd and much fun and games, with the group having won and everything. There wasn't a single cloud on our horizon.

We returned home on Sunday and Mam and Dad were waiting for us by the gate, something that never happens. Something must have been amiss. Dad is a hard man, never showing much emotion, but he was obviously upset.

'Keith is dead,' he said.

Hearing his words was like a blow to the stomach. Keith, who was like a big brother to me. Keith, who was with Uncle Teg everywhere. Keith, who worked on the mountain and sheared with us. Keith, who was like one of the family. Keith dead. He'd been found dead in his bed on the Saturday night as we were enjoying ourselves in Bala.

I had the fright of my life. But that wasn't all. Another friend of mine, Jason Jones, was killed on his motorbike on the Friday night. Jason met up with us in the local pub on Saturday nights before we all went to Bangor when we were young. Richard, my cousin, was his best friend and had to go to identify his body.

The following Friday we were burying both. I was one of the bearers at Keith's funeral, the family man with a wife, Gwyneth and the twins, two little girls. And I, not thinking straight, unable to get my head around the circumstances, a young life gone, one with whom I had done so much. I was feeling very low, realising at the same time that in the next hour I would be at Jason's funeral. Two friends dying on consecutive nights with their burial services on the same day at Horeb Chapel.

The first week in August 1997. Great experiences in Bala, and then losing two friends. Two great losses shutting the door of happiness in my face.

But that's life isn't it? The good and the bad, the happy and the sad. Up to now I've had more of the happy than the sad, and for that I am grateful.